Inspired Living - Faith-Filled Reflections for a Life Without Limitations, Volume II

Written by Anita Sechesky

Copyright © 2020 LWL PUBLISHING HOUSE
A division of: Anita Sechesky – Living Without Limitations Inc.

All rights reserved. No part of this publication may be reproduced, distributed or transmitted in any form or by any means, including photocopying, recording, or other electronic or mechanical methods without prior written permission of the publisher, except in the case of brief quotations embodied in critical reviews and certain other noncommercial uses permitted by copyright law. For permission requests, write to the publisher, addressed "Attention: Permissions Coordinator," at the address below.
LWL PUBLISHING HOUSE uses American Standard English in our publications.

Anita Sechesky – Living Without Limitations Inc.
16 Rutherford Road South,
Brampton, ON L6W 3J1
Email: lwlclienthelp@gmail.com
Website: www.lwlpublishinghouse.com

LEGAL DISCLAIMER: This book does not replace a pastor, minister, church leader, counsellor, health professional, or a Certified Professional Coach, but can be used by any Christian woman as a learning tool to motivate themselves throughout the year.

The information and content contained within this book does not substitute any form of professional counsel such as a Psychologist, Physician, Pastor/Minister, Life Coach, or Counselor. The contents and information provided does not constitute professional or legal advice in any way, shape or form.

All written material is a reflection of the author's vision, faith, and insight, based on her personal life and professional experiences, at her discretion. Anita Sechesky, Anita Sechesky – Living Without Limitations Inc. or LWL PUBLISHING HOUSE is not liable for any misrepresentations, false or unknown statements, actions, or judgments made by any of the contents in this book. This book was created in good faith to encourage others.

Any decisions you make, and the outcomes thereof are entirely your own doing. Under no circumstances can you hold the author, LWL PUBLISHING HOUSE, or "Anita Sechesky – Living Without Limitations Inc." liable for any actions that you take. You agree not to hold the author, LWL PUBLISHING HOUSE, or "Anita Sechesky – Living Without Limitations Inc." liable for any loss or expense incurred by you, as a result of materials, advice, coaching, or mentoring offered within. The tools and activities offered in this book are strategies used when working with a Certified Professional Coach and are intended to be self-motivating with respect to real life issues and are offered in good faith; however, you are under no obligation to utilize these motivational tools.

Nothing contained in this book shall be considered legal, financial, or actuarial advice.

The author and Publisher assume no liability or responsibility for the outcome from your results of using this publication.

It may introduce what a Certified Professional Coach, Counselor, Pastor/Minister or Therapist may discuss with you at any given time during personal sessions. The content contained herein is not meant to replace the Professional roles of a physician or any of the above-mentioned professions.

Book Layout © 2020 LWL PUBLISHING HOUSE

Inspired Living - Faith-Filled Reflections for a Life Without Limitations, Volume II
Anita Sechesky – Living Without Limitations
ISBN 978-1-988867-76-2

Book Cover Design: N. Sechesky
Inside Layout: LWL PUBLISHING HOUSE Editorial Team

Table of Contents

Dedication	2
In Gratitude	3
Introduction	4
God's Promises	5
Dear Soul Sister	6
Love for the Greater Good	7
Inspired Living Pages	8 to 15
Dear Sisters of the World	16
Inspired Living Pages	19 to 23
Love & Friendship	24
Inspired Living Pages	30 to 34
Abundance Mindset	35
Inspired Living Pages	40 to 44
Divine Purpose	45
Inspired Living Pages	49 to 52
Self-Love & Development	53
Inspired Living Pages	57 to 60
Faith Walk	61
Inspired Living Pages	65 to 69
No Greater Love	70
Inspired Living Pages	74 to 88

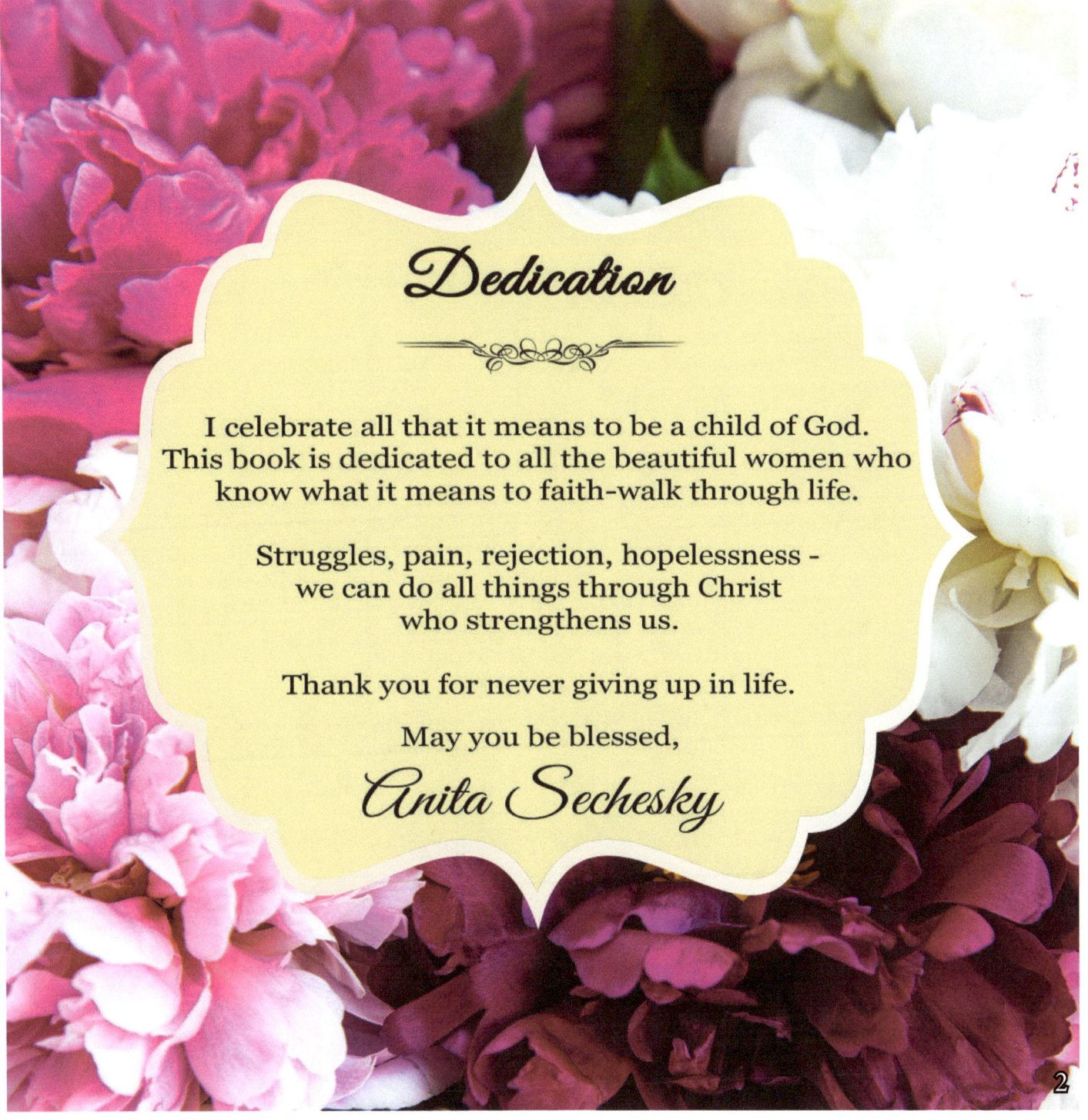

Dedication

I celebrate all that it means to be a child of God.
This book is dedicated to all the beautiful women who
know what it means to faith-walk through life.

Struggles, pain, rejection, hopelessness -
we can do all things through Christ
who strengthens us.

Thank you for never giving up in life.

May you be blessed,

Anita Sechesky

In Joyful Gratitude

Special Thanks of Gratitude to God, my Heavenly Father. It is because of you that I can do all things. May it always be pleasing to you.

My children, Nathaniel & Sammy - You are my special blessings. Everything I do is for both of you.

My hubby, Stephen - Thank you for your loving support and dedication to see Volume II of this project to completion.

My Mom & Dad, Jean & Jetty Seergobin - I'm so honored to be your daughter. Thank you for all that you are to me.

My brother Trevor & sis-in-love Myka - Thank you for the joyful love you bring into our family.

LWL Media Support Team - You are the best! Thank you for perfecting this beautiful book.

An extra special thanks to all my family, friends, former patients, nursing colleagues & clients - each of you have helped to inspire the vision of this book series.

Introduction

The vision for this book was inspired by the life events that I faced and overcame throughout the years. My vision grew bigger as I also experienced life through the eyes of my patients, colleagues, clients & personal relationships. There are chapters excerpted from *Soul Sister Letters* and *Love Your Life* to help you be inspired in your faith-walk.

It became apparent to me that even though we will always face trials and tribulations in this life, we can still learn to invite healing and set ourselves free from so many struggles and limiting beliefs.

Our souls cry for peace and we must find the true source to become all we were created to be. I trust that you will find something within these pages to bring comfort in your times of need.

Many Blessings,

Anita Sechesky

God's Promises

Exodus 14:14 - *The Lord will fight for you; you need only to be still.*

Psalms 23:4 - *Even though I walk through the darkest valley, I will fear no evil for You are with me. Your rod and your staff, they comfort me.*

Psalms 37:4 - *Take delight in the LORD and He will give you the desires of your heart.*

Psalms 139: 13-14 - *For You created my inmost being; you knit me together in my mother's womb. I praise you because I am fearfully and wonderfully made.*

Proverbs 3: 5-6 - *Trust in the LORD with all your heart and lean not on your own understanding. In all your ways submit to Him and He will make your paths straight.*

Isaiah 40:29 - *He gives strength to the weary and increases the power of the weak.*

Jeremiah 29:11 - *For I know the plans I have for you declares the LORD, plans to proper you and not to harm you, plans to give you a hope and a future.*

Mark 11:24 - *Therefore I tell you whatever you ask for in prayer, believe you have received it, and it will be yours.*

John 3:16 - *For God so loved the world that He gave His one and only Son, that whoever believes in Him shall not perish, but have eternal life.*

Romans 8:28 - *And we know that in all things, God works for the good of those who love Him, those who have been called according to His purpose.*

Philippians 4:19 - *And my God will meet all your needs according to His riches in glory.*

2 Timothy 1:7 - *For God did not give us a spirit of fear, but of power, love, and a sound mind.*

Dear Soul Sister;

I believe in the beauty of who you are. That's why I was inspired to create this faith-filled, inspirational planner & prayer life journal just for you. I know what it's like to have big goals, small goals, and no one to speak into my life to accomplish any of them. I also know what it's like to actually hit those goals and the joy it brings.

I pray that as you actively push yourself to work through the following pages this year, the Holy Spirit will inspire you to also see God's plans and purposes for you: to prosper and bless you with no added stress.

Remember, to accomplish anything in life, we must have a winning and forgiving mindset – from beginning to end.
There is no time for distractions when we have a purpose-driven life.

2021 is the year of personal growth and healing.
I pray that as you journal and plan throughout the following days and months ahead, you'll also draw closer to God, your Heavenly Father, who's got you in the palms of His hands.

Onward to Triumphant Victory!

Anita Sechesky

Love for the Greater Good

by Anita Sechesky

When was the last time a friend told you everything that you needed to know to be happy, successful, and satisfied with the life that you have? It's not very often that we can find such a friend as this who will tell us where and how to change our lives to get exactly what we want. That's why I've created this book so that when you're going through struggles and difficulties, or contemplating your personal value and learning that life is not exactly the way that you thought it would be, you can reach for this book and find reasons to keep believing in yourself.

I have gone through moments of feeling inadequate, insignificant, or not appreciated. I really believe that each one of us walks through these moments. Some people know how to manage this energy a lot better than others and what I mean is those individuals understand how to raise their vibration energy. The conscious awareness of appreciating that everything is energy around me has significantly impacted the way I view life and all the experiences that I walk through. As a person of faith, my foundation of belief is derived from the teachings that God created the Universe by the power of His words and everything in it including His Universal Laws[1]. These include:

The Law of Divine Oneness – Everything is connected and affects all.

The Law of Vibration – Everything moves and vibrates with its own unique frequency.

The Law of Action – We must choose activities that support the outcome we desire.

The Law of Correspondence – The Laws of physics takes into consideration the energy of light, vibration, and motion to create a physical world.

The Law of Cause and Effect – Every thought and word has a consequence. Nothing randomly happens by chance.

The Law of Compensation – The Law of Cause and Effect applied to the overflow of blessings as rewards of our actions.

The Law of Attraction – Our positive or negative thoughts and actions attract people and experiences with the same vibrational energies.

The Law of Perpetual Transmutation of Energy – When you understand the Universal Laws and how they can work for you, you have the power to change your life based on your own thoughts, prayers, words, actions, and reactions.

The Law of Relativity – Everything we experience, feel, and see is a result of comparing it in relation to something already existing in this world.

The Law of Polarity – This law is also known as the Law of Mental Vibration because we have the ability to control our thoughts that will put into action the life we desire.

The Law of Rhythm – Everything is in constant motion because of God's Universal regularity of life as we know it, such as the seasons, stages of development, cycles, and patterns.

The Law of Gender – This law guides all of creation. For life to transpire and flourish, everything in nature exists as either masculine or feminine.

[1] Retrieved from https://lawsoftheuniverse.weebly.com/12-immutable-universal-laws.html

The words that we speak are energy and affect the people that we choose to be around. It adds to our vibration or it takes away from our energy by the emotion that results from our interactions. The same can be said about the people we are constantly around; they can add to our vitality and life energy or they can drain us by the way they treat us. That's why relationships are a direct reflection of how we see ourselves because we chose who is in our lives and how they are towards us. Although we cannot choose our families, we can still manage our interactions and how we allow our conversations to be. The choices we make and the things that we participate in life on a daily basis determines the kind of energy that we will feel when we are involved in activities. So today I want you to think about what kind of energy you want to be. High, healthy, and happy vibration that attracts all good things, people, and experiences into your life…or the opposite – a low vibration that can show up as feelings of sadness, complacency, allowing yourself to focus on what didn't work out, or anything that results in lack, rejection, and emptiness? Who wants that? Especially when you understand you get to choose what you want in life.

Always remember that although energy is instant, the vibrational thoughts around you will have to become filtered, and you need to consciously choose different thought patterns if you want different results in life. It's also important to remember, if you want to start applying the principles of praying or meditating in your life, you will need to stay focused and hold your emotions on what you are believing for. This means no more doubting or allowing yourself to get distracted with the past experiences that didn't make you happy. Instead, you need to start allowing yourself to imagine more. What does it feel like to have what you want? Hold those thoughts more often, meaning that I encourage you to actually time yourself holding a thought in your mind for longer than a minute so that it becomes a habit. Your subconscious mind will reach for that positive thought vibration more often than the negative ones that resulted in unhappiness. In fact, I would like you to try an exercise as you begin reading this book. Hold the thought of how much you love yourself for one whole minute, four times a day. Continue doing this until you feel a difference in the way you look at life.

What kind of energy is going to make you feel good about yourself? How do you increase your energy? How do you raise your awareness to see how special you really are? We don't need people to validate that we are important. We've been conditioned to believe that we must be accepted by certain people, and when that happens that's when we become important, valued, appreciated, and significant. I strongly believe this is the wrong way to look at life. Each one of us has value. God saw value when he created us, and because He is God, we are perfectly made. Our imperfections are a result of wear and tear in a world that places value on the material things in life instead of the spiritual things. Can you imagine how different life would be if we could see the motives of a person's heart and the intentions they had towards us? God knew that we were going to bring value to the people that are around us. I believe the situations we walk through determine the kind of people we are by the choices we make. We can choose to show up how we want and look at life from a positive perspective because we are optimistic, or we can allow the past to keep defining our future. I believe that no one is perfect in this world and no one has ever been born into a perfect family. I encourage you to hold on and not give up despite your circumstances.

This book was created for my fellow sisters around the world. Know that you are important, valued, and perfect just the way you are. It's not about a monetary value, it's not about a social status, it's not about what you can give. I truly understand that to live your best life, you must love the life that you have first. You must love it enough to make a change. You must love that you have the opportunity to make choices. You must love that you can evolve every day. You must first see how precious you are and accept all of your shortcomings and flaws. You see, everything that you have looked down upon in your own life is a result of comparing yourself to others. Once you start accepting who you are and how you look at the world, you can recognize that the greatness you've been seeking has always been within you. My prayer is that you would learn to love your life again and live your life without limitations. All it takes is for you to make that decision and walking it through.

I have carefully written this book so that it will help you step into a new level of confidence in your life. You will be able to recognize how self-sabotaging behaviors can quickly derail your personal or professional goals and learn how to stay focused despite emotional and personal challenges along the way.

I have proven this perspective to be true through my growth and development. You see, I did not understand the concept of being present or mindful through some of my past experiences. I used to get distracted by everything around me and did not put my life as a top priority. Many things got pushed to the wayside and I ended up feeling discouraged with myself for setting such high expectations when I knew I was "busy." Of course, I was busy with two young children, a hubby, a fur baby, and working a full-time shift position with my nursing career that totally messed up my circadian rhythm. However, I finally learned the value of who I was by looking at myself through God's eyes and appreciating that He accepted me already despite all my failures and shortcomings.

Today, it is my greatest desire that you will find the hope, inspiration, and motivation to beat any form of procrastination, doubts, or fears that are currently holding you back from living your best life ever! When you wake up to the understanding that your self-talk is the biggest barrier to leading the life you most deserve, nothing can stop you from being consciously aware of how special you are. You deserve to LOVE the life you're living.

CHILD OF GOD...*be bold for the Lord thy God is with thee. You have authority in Jesus name to be set free from hatred, jealousy, animosity, fear, rejection, trauma, abuse, racism, spitefulness, and so much more.*

SAY OUT LOUD: *THE BLOOD OF JESUS is against every thought, word, or curse spoken against me and the anointing that God has placed on my life to bless others with. Anything and anyone that tries to defile the will of God for me will be held accountable in Jesus mighty name.*

NO WEAPON FORMED: *I put every wayward thought into captivity and cover myself and every person reading this prayer with the blood of Jesus.*

SAY OUT LOUD: *I will not be used by the enemy to create division, destruction, or delay in my life or anyone else's life any longer.*

SAY OUT LOUD: *I BIND THE WORKS OF THE ENEMY operating in my life and the lives of people who know me personally or know of me. I cast out to dry places anything that is not of God. I send back to Sender everything that is not a blessing for me to where it came from.*

RECEIVE YOUR DELIVERANCE NOW *in Jesus mighty name! Hallelujah! You deserve a blessed and prosperous life filled with love, joy, peace, health, wholeness, and vitality.*

Read Psalm 91

Amen!

Anita Sechesky

**Excerpted from *Love Your Life – Inspiration to Motivate You for Living a Life Without Limitations*

*You are
creating
the world
around you
by the beauty
in your words.*

~Anita Sechesky

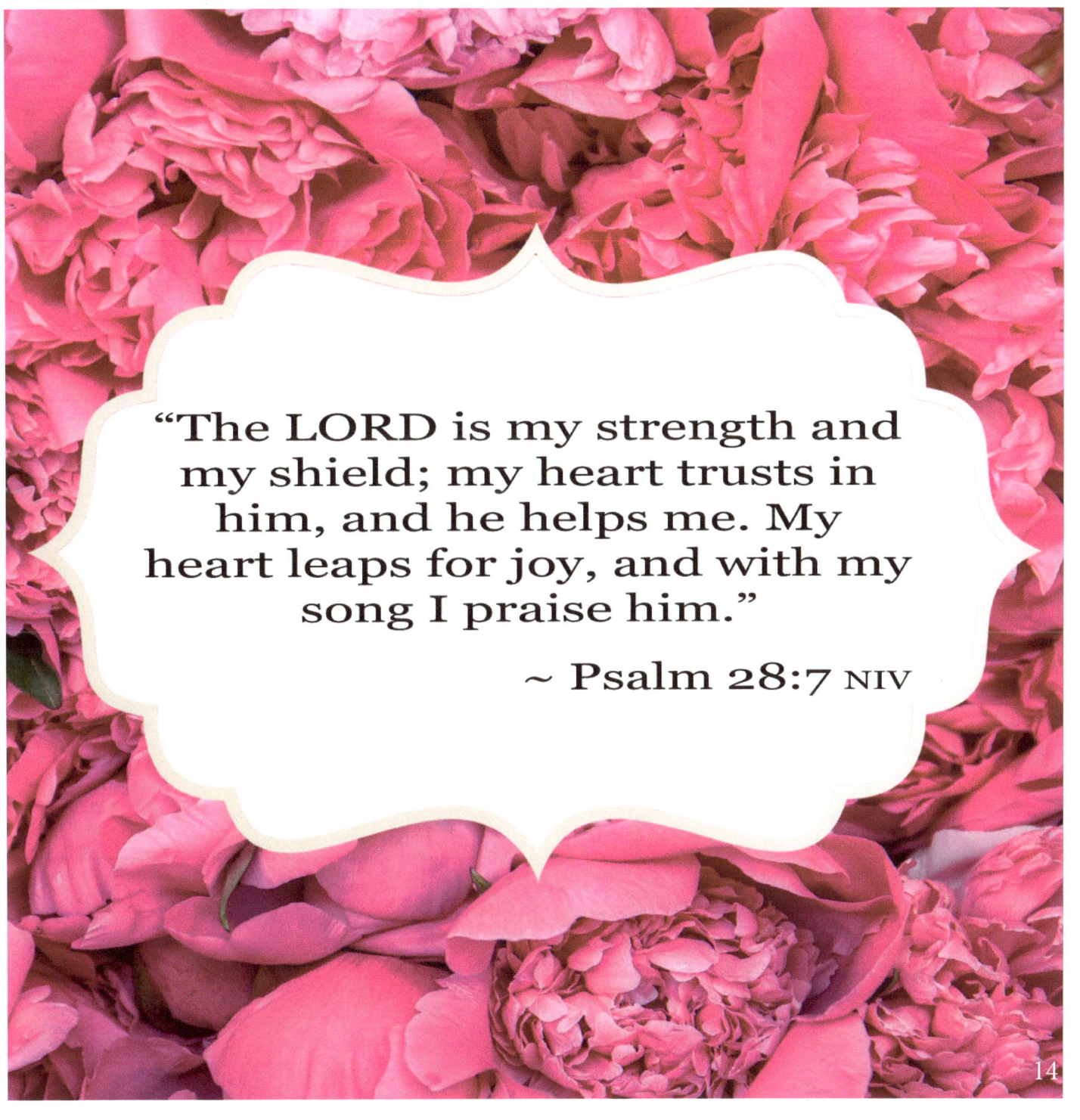

"The LORD is my strength and my shield; my heart trusts in him, and he helps me. My heart leaps for joy, and with my song I praise him."

~ Psalm 28:7 NIV

Dear Sisters of the World

by Anita Sechesky

If you knew how amazing you are, you would never allow another person to ever hurt you again. You must know the people who belittle and cause destruction in the souls of others are bitter and broken with no love and compassion for themselves. As we show mercy and empathy for those around us, our hearts have a greater purpose to bring healing for everyone. The way people project their emotions is quite often a reflection of what's happening within them. Life is not always how we expect it to be and there are days you may feel like throwing in the towel. It's in those moments that I encourage you to step back and reflect on how far you've already come. Sure, there may still be a long way to go to achieve your goals. But your journey has always shown you the depth of your dreams, even though you still can't see the bigger picture as it beautifully, and yes sometimes painfully, unfolds before you. You will always find your strength within if you seek a higher power such as God, the Creator, and Heavenly Father. It's amazing what a simple prayer cried out in times of struggle and surrender can do for your broken spirit and lost soul in a world of hate, contempt, and jealousy.

I implore you to never be hard on yourselves and don't take out your frustrations on the very people who care so deeply for you. They are hurting just as you are when things don't work out as you anticipated. The loved ones we have close to us are the people who feel the deepest desire to see us succeed. Give them a little more compassion and patience for they are not purposely driven by the passion and God source you may be following. In fact, they just believe in you, just as you are. They don't ask questions, instead they just willingly give of themselves to help bring your dreams to life.

It's not always easy to love someone with a deep commitment for something bigger than self, just like it's not always easy to understand why others are jealous, spiteful, and lacking appreciation and acceptance of who we are.

You will find that life presents you with so many opportunities to connect with multitudes of individuals, but please have wisdom and guard your precious and beating heart. It's in the very moments of inspiring others at their starting points in life that you may stir up something ugly in someone who will never appreciate the knowledge, encouragement, and inspiration you freely pour into them. You see, it's already inside of them Their own ugliness becomes mixed with the jealousy that grows as they witness you striving and jumping over hoops and high towers – you suddenly became a target for competition. They will try to use your naivety and kindness to reap as much information from you. And when things are exposed into your spirit of who exactly they are, they will conveniently lose you to someone else that's up and coming or eagerly looking for someone to follow. Like attracts like, so this is a good thing when you lose those so-called "friends" because they never really were friends. In fact, I would refer to individuals like that as "fiends who suck out the positive energy from you." They glean as much as they can before exiting your life as painfully as possible. Don't let them get that chance to hurt you. Know who they are now and release! Release! Release! Then start focusing on all the love that surrounds you. You are loved and appreciated by so many; why be discouraged any longer by the few who were never meant to be a part of your life. We each evolve and are still growing into our true authentic and loving self. It's your time to continue your journey without any limitations of negativity.

There will come a time when you will see "flashing lights" around certain people I have just described, but unfortunately not until a few have made their way onto your path so you can learn to identify their selfish and false personalities immediately. I have learned quite quickly that when people tell you they were divinely sent to build you up or take you to that next level, it's time to arm all your security systems on the Homefront. From my own experience, they always show up loud and leave loud and proud. Sadly, they will never achieve what they are after because of their lack of wisdom and integrity. This shortcoming will always hold them back until they make things right and release their own personal past identities in exchange for a clean and clear conscience.

For you my dear sisters of the world, you should know you have the right and freedom to own your emotions, strengths, and creativity. Allow yourselves to be divinely guided and never permit something to block your perception of how to live a life without limitations. You dreamed it and now it's time to achieve it!

Love Your Life,

Anita Sechesky

**Excerpted from *Soul Sister Letters – Let's Talk About Love, Faith, Abundance & Divine Purpose*

Prayer for Increased Faith

Dearest Heavenly Father;

Today I ask that you will take my mustard seed faith and increase it so that your will be done in my life. Help me to stand on your promises to believe that no weapon formed against me shall prosper and every tongue raised up against me shall be condemned in your name.
As your child, I'm asking for more of your presence in my life. I ask and I thank you for this in your precious and Holy Name.

Amen.

*Life is more
precious
when you
see your
humanity
reflected
in everyone.*

-Anita Sechesky

"But the Lord is faithful, and he will strengthen you and protect you from the evil one."

~ 2 Thessalonians 3:3 NIV

Love & Friendship

by Anita Sechesky

Dear Sis; Life is not always what it seems like when it comes to Love and Friendship. I really want to help you understand how I feel about the things I have walked through in my own life. You see, I believe that many times we are so caught up in who we are at that moment that we forget to guard our hearts. As a result, I have found that there are so many similarities when it comes to romantic love and friendships that I felt it was time we give ourselves permission to talk about it in context.

With romantic love, we allow ourselves the opportunity to bare our hearts and souls to an individual we do not necessarily know everything about because we want to be loved and cared for by someone who we feel connected with. Therefore, we are not being fully aware of the great risk we are taking yet believe nothing bad will ever happen. This very risk is adventurous and exhilarating at the very least because it comes with a range of new experiences that will help us to feel good about life and who we are. On the flip side, although we cannot predict the future, we will find ourselves in situations where we realize that this person is not for us because they don't hold the same passions, dreams, or are not interested in making things work out for the best. At that moment, we know it's over but sometimes struggle with letting go. Always hoping for the best and downgrading our feelings, we believe we're the problem or the reason things are not going well. Eventually, the truth does come out and we stop the madness.

Yes, we mentally and physically let go, but emotionally we still hold on to so many issues about the memories of what didn't work because, as females, we tend to overplay and analyze things in our heads instead of releasing what didn't serve our highest good. All of this goes back to our conditioning as young girls and how we learned that we needed to be proper girls and not tomboys. We had to behave and dress a certain way. I'm not sure if anything is actually wrong with this concept, however, what concerns me as a Christian and Certified Professional Coach, as well as a health care provider, is the missing information in between, such as it's okay to be exactly as you are but know that you are also fearfully and wonderfully made in the image of Christ. If God says you are perfect, then believe it! You are perfect.

Jesus had twelve disciples or friends, and even He experienced deception when Judas turned against him. Jesus loved His friends; He shared His adult life's journey with them day by day. They traveled together, did ministry together, and ate together. They were in each other's faces 24/7! They spoke into each other's lives…in fact, they were so committed to serving Jesus they left the lives they were living to join His vision! So, tell me what does your tribe look like? What are they giving up so they can join forces with your bigger picture vision? Are they truly supporting you or are they just waving a flag on the sidelines waiting for the next opportunity to come along for them?

I honestly believe that we are meant to have friends that are closer than a brother/sibling; friends who love us enough to die for us; stand by us and never throw in the towel because they can see the vision in our hearts.

Know this: that when your vision is for the greater good, the right people will always find their way into your life. I have personally experienced the deception of allowing myself to become too desperate because of the words that were spoken. Another thing to remember, God does give us the desires of our hearts according to His riches in glory. It's His word and this we can depend on as believers.

I quickly learned that sometimes words people speak are as cheap as that same person who speaks them. Be mindful of who you allow speaking into your life and their motives. You can test this theory by the fruit they have already produced and the history of their walk… ask and keep asking. Look out for patterns and understand where they are coming from. If they make you feel like you cannot do anything without their input, yet they have nothing to show for it in their own lives...be wary. If they tell you what they think and criticize you without considering your own positive experiences...be wary. If they undermine your efforts and tell you they know better or have a better way of doing things...be wary if once again they have nothing to show for it. You might be kind, courteous, and generous in all your ways, but you were not made to be someone's doormat. Real friends never take advantage of each other. They are always trying to out give and bless each other; no competition and no keeping scores. They have something called loyalty and wear it proudly on their chest. They respect that you have worked hard to build something with your own hands, and they are going to stick around forever, not drop you when someone more exciting comes along. They keep you in the loop and encourage you to grow so you can become the best version of yourself. They are not deceptive, looking for ways they can take advantage of your kindness. They will protect you and your good name when you are not around. That is love.

I can say this: I'm so saddened when I hear stories of genuinely kind-hearted sisters being taken for. Vulnerability is no joke. As women of God, many of us wear our hearts on our sleeves, so we become sitting ducks for individuals who are looking for opportunities to piggyback off of our success without a second thought. I encourage you, Sister, to cover yourself with the Blood of Jesus and take everything in prayer when it comes to all your relationships. Trust me, you will feel the discomfort of disloyal people in your life and question it, but feel that you are thinking wrongly of that person. It's because of God's pure light and love within you. The darkness or sin cannot stand the light. All things do eventually come into the light and are exposed as they are taken into captivity. We must remember the Holy Spirit and what it means to be a child of God. This is real and God is our comforter and protector by giving us thoughts that guide us away from harm's way, regardless of whether it is a romantic relationship or friendship. I truly believe that's also why God wants us to wait for that special relationship with another believer so we don't have to go through so many emotional disasters testing the waters with people who are not meant to trample our spirits and damage us. If this happens, it would be so easy for us to be pulled away from the plans that God has for our lives; those same plans I've read about are in the Bible that states God wants us to prosper us and not bring harm to us. Plus, the BONUS of that awesome man coming into our lives, who was created in God's image, and is absolutely perfect for us!

So, my dear Sisters in Christ, it's up to us to pay attention to what we are sensing. There really is no other way to describe it as a child of God. We must take all things into prayer so we are never steered wrong by the desires of our hearts, whether it's about fitting in with our peers or finding the perfect guy.

Allow the lessons to be learned. Forgive and release those individuals and then move on. Your pain will heal, and it will also be replaced with joy as you keep hold of your strong faith. I encourage you to embrace the fact that nothing is perfect in this world, but we can find peace, hope, healing, love, friendship, and success in every area of our lives.

The same goes for female friendships. We do connect deeply with our sister friends initially because of emotions in many cases, then we learn quickly what's positive and what's negative about each friendship. Maybe it becomes one-sided. We always have to support them emotionally with every issue that comes up and we stand strong to defend them until one day we realize that the other people were not wrong – our dear sister is unhealed and damaged and we have become an accomplice to their misery and grief. This is a huge eye-opener because we are not narcissistic or vengeful but many things that once seemed fun are staring us in the face and we understand that is not who we are. Or we find ourselves becoming their bank account with too many free withdrawals that never get paid back or they are always borrowing our personal items, such as clothes, shoes, purses, etc.

You see, anytime we have to become vulnerable and trust another, it ultimately seeps into so many other areas of our lives and we find ourselves unexpectantly in icky situations that we were not emotionally prepared to deal with. I have learned in my own journey that it can either become crippling or empowering and this is something that only we can determine for ourselves. Thank goodness God only gives us the lesson until we have learned it and the cycle stops after that. The interesting thing about that is I can clearly remember situations where I had similar experiences with different so-called friendships and I quickly set into motion the quality of my thoughts to that of least resistance. I recognized my patterns and adapted into what kind of outcome I was seeking because I learned very early in life that we cannot change anyone to like us or support us. I realized through so many personal failures and disappointments that people will determine who they want to support and who they want to embrace as their own. I had to be the one who was seeing the best in me. I had to learn to be my own BFF (Best Friend Forever). Please don't get me wrong, I have always had friends, and having friends was never an issue in my life because of my outgoing personality. I find joy in everything.

My real friends that truly cared about me listened to my issues, cared about my feelings, understood my pain, brought fun, good memories and lots of great experiences into my life as I also reciprocated it back into their lives. I can honestly say I am thankful for those life-long friendships that remain even though we have grown up and gone our separate ways…I believe we still hold a special place for one another in each other's hearts.

The thing about me was that I also learned this lesson while living it out – you cannot change anyone to like you. You can only change yourself. So, I decided that since I was going to be the only one I could truly depend on, I better start appreciating some things about myself. I better start getting over being Bulimic in high school when only one of my close friends told me that she didn't want me to harm myself any longer. I didn't even know I was doing anything wrong. I just wanted to be skinny. I wanted to be perfect. I wanted to be accepted and liked and popular, which was a next-to-impossible thing to achieve in a small Northwestern Ontario community – I was the ethnic girl; I was the brown girl; I was the black girl. I was the one who didn't fit in. I was the one who stood out. I was the one that my friends who knew and loved me just as I am, couldn't understand why I wanted to be different. You see, when you are part of a small group, you become comfortable. You can feel protected in a sense from the harshness of the world, but in reality, the bigger picture doesn't let you forget. They will still look at you indifferently. They can be in your school, your community groups, even your church. This is life. People will always place you into categories. It will affect your friendships and relationships. I hope this changes for the better, for you.

My younger days were so awesome. I feel I had the best of friends growing up. They never made me feel like an outsider just because I was born in Guyana, South America. However, I recall a time when I had spent a year of Junior high school living in Calgary with relatives to gain a bigger world view. When I returned home at the end of the school year, I felt the shift in how my friends viewed me. Some of them had the struggle to accept me back. Some said I was boasting about my experience. Some said I was just different. You see, in that short time away from my hometown, I quickly understood what was missing from my life and why I felt so trapped and limited. I was a product of my small-town environment who didn't have a world view of who exactly I was in Christ. That had put me in a place of insignificance for so many years. It was the perfect time in my life to actually be exposed to this reality and understand that no matter what others thought of me, their small-minded limiting beliefs about me were just a projection of themselves and I did not ever have to accept it as my own! Talk about a profound awakening! Thank you, Jesus! Unfortunately, I had allowed the way others viewed me in a limited capacity to affect so much about who I was growing up to be. Of course, it affected all my relationships and the biggest, most significant relationship was with myself and how I saw who I was. My world expanded and I suddenly saw that I was not the only brown girl in the world. I learned for the first time that being a brown girl was actually beautiful. I was introduced to other brown-skinned friends who loved me exactly as I was, once again. But for some reason, this time it really did feel different and more impactful because we reflected each other in our skins. Now that I've addressed the skin thing, I will admit it is the saddest thing because we miss out on so many beautiful friendships. As for me, my husband is Caucasian, and I see no difference in who he is as my life partner, father of my children, and best friend.

However, the greatest lesson I have learned about female friendships and the vulnerability of opening our hearts to love our friends as sisters is that we all carry preconceived ideas of who our ideal friend is and should be. We hold biases against people without knowing their hearts, motives, the significant impact they could have on our lives, and how we can positively impact theirs. Women, we just role differently amongst each other.

Therefore, as a follower of Christ, it leads me to question if we really understand that the skin thing is a much more serious issue and once we transition from this realm, we are dropping our skins. So, will we even recognize each other in Heaven, if that is our only focus, and not looking at our hearts instead?

Anita Sechesky

**Excerpted from *Soul Sister Letters – Let's Talk About Love, Faith, Abundance & Divine Purpose*

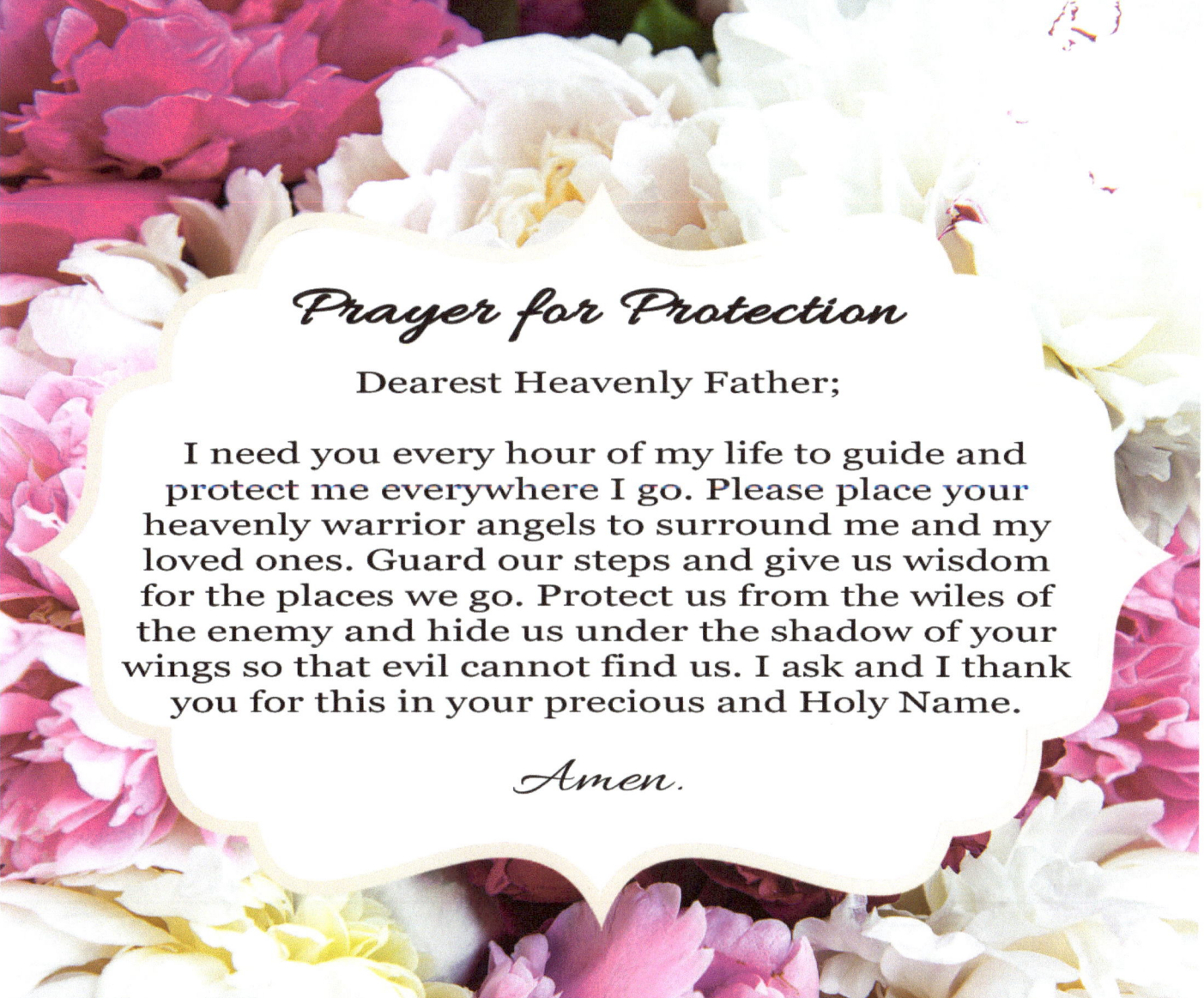

Prayer for Protection

Dearest Heavenly Father;

I need you every hour of my life to guide and protect me everywhere I go. Please place your heavenly warrior angels to surround me and my loved ones. Guard our steps and give us wisdom for the places we go. Protect us from the wiles of the enemy and hide us under the shadow of your wings so that evil cannot find us. I ask and I thank you for this in your precious and Holy Name.

Amen.

Everthing in my life is a blessing: the good, the bad & the yucky because I get to choose how it will benefit me.

~Anita Sechesky

"The Lord will fight for you; you need only to be still."

~ Exodus 14:14 NIV

Abundance Mindset

by Anita Sechesky

Dear Sis; How's it going in the manifestation department lately? Have you been limiting yourself in how you see life? Don't despair because it's not too late for you to shift the way you are allowing life's blessings from passing you by.

As a Law of Attraction practitioner, I can tell you that everything begins with your thoughts. So, if your thoughts are tainted with deep roots of discouragement from past failures or rejection, more than likely you are still struggling with self-esteem and how you show up in the world.

Firstly, let me point you to scripture:

> "And my God will supply every need of yours according to his riches in glory in Christ Jesus." Philippians 4:19 (EVS)

> "For I know the plans I have for you, declares the Lord, plans for welfare and not for evil, to give you a future and a hope." Jeremiah 29:11 (ESV)

> "Blessed is the man who walks not in the counsel of the wicked, nor stands in the way of sinners, nor sits in the seat of scoffers, but his delight is in the law of the Lord, and on his law, he meditates day and night. He is like a tree planted by streams of water that yields its fruit in its season, and its leaf does not wither. In all that he does, he prospers." Psalm 1:1-3 (ESV)

My Sisters, there are literally hundreds of passages in the Holy Bible that indicate we are blessed and have access to all the blessings that God has prepared for us as his children.

So why do we keep thinking otherwise? Why do we struggle? Why do we lack? Are we being punished?

I have asked myself these same questions so many times, and then God brings to remembrance that sweet solid truth that yes, God has called me as His very own. But it's the sin in my life that's actually blocking my blessings. This prompts me in the busyness of my life to wake up and take notice that once again in my weak humanness, I stepped out of God's will for my life failing to repent and asking forgiveness. Even forgiving others who have wronged me may have opened the door of sin in my life because I started harboring ill feelings against someone. It is so easy to not walk a righteous life and yet it just as easy to walk joyfully in the presence of the Lord. I say this boldly knowing my own shortcomings and personal attitude when it comes to the Abundance mindset. We tend to shift our focus and look to others who are at the top of their game. Success seems to follow them so easily and we wonder what's wrong with us? Why is it always this way?

I have personally learned the biggest game-changer is when we realize what we focus on is literally what we are attracting into our lives. For example, what are you feeding your mind on a daily basis? Who are you listening to? Who are you following on social media? Whose books are you reading? When was the last time you did any kind of personal growth training? Have you processed and released all your emotional baggage?

Let's break it down so we can examine ourselves in a productive way.

If I asked you what you do on a daily basis in the morning, what category would you fit into?

- read scripture devotionals
- listen to worship music
- get into prayer mode and lay it all on the cross
- declare blessings over my household

What we feed our minds and the secret to our success is always found in our daily routines.

I encourage you to reflect on this momentarily and if you know you have been procrastinating and then complaining or holding negative thoughts inside because you wish you were living differently, it's not too late. Forgive yourself and release all forms of malice towards anyone in your life that you may actually be jealous of. Instead, start looking at everyone and everything differently because old stagnant emotions will keep attracting itself back into your life. You want to take that trash out as soon as you are consciously aware of it. You will then notice that your energy will shift because you are looking through different lenses. You see, once you recognize that God is no respecter of person and what He has done for others, He can also do for you, you will realize that no one is better than another. Jesus died for all of our sins, not just your neighbor across the street. Your life is just as valuable and important. So that means the quality of your life as well. God wants us all to prosper and be of good health. The bible says that he wants us to prosper as our souls prosper. I believe God's word to be true and acceptable in my life. I am well aware of my humanity and where I fall short because of my lack of seeking God in all my ways. I know it always feels heavy and uncomfortable if I allow myself to become jealous or spiteful. We are not immune to these feelings, but it's also our responsibility to put these thoughts into immediate captivity and not let them run rampant in our minds, which is our greatest battle. The enemy of our souls may plant seeds of contempt against others and because of our vulnerability by not clearing our minds and building our faith in prayer, we are prone to going down a rabbit hole of sin, and with that usually comes discouragement in many forms.

I believe we tend to make things so much more difficult than our Heavenly Father intended things to be. We have issues with trust and as a result, because we do not see a physical God before us, we easily slip up and forget that because of the very fact that God is not a man, He will not lie to us.

> *"God is not a man, that he should lie; Neither the son of man, that he should repent: hath he said and shall he not do it?"* Numbers 23:19 (KJV)

It's time for us all to stand on God's word and meditate on it for what it is: B – basic, I – information, B – before, L – leaving, E – earth.

An interesting thing about life as a Christian: it's often been said that life doesn't come with a manual, but as a child of God, we hold contrary to that statement as we have access to the Keys of the Kingdom living. This means as joint heirs in Christ Jesus, as children of God, we are abundantly blessed whether we believe it or not. It's our inheritance and it's time we start living as just so. We must cast off all vain imaginations and trust God's word as it is. We must recognize that to reap good fruit we must sow into good soil. We must fertilize our bodies, minds, and spirits on the Word and promises of God. We must forgive often and release all sin that tries to stick itself onto us.

We can definitely do all things through Christ, but do we actually believe this to be true? If I were to observe you, what would I see? Are you confident? Are you generous? Are you thinking of the needs of others? Do you sow love and blessings in every life you are connected with?

I encourage you, Sis, to continually clean your mind of all the things that have not edified your beautiful soul. Release all the words that have been spoken over any kind of success or prosperity in your life. Forgive every single person who has ever betrayed your trust. Process the steps over and ask God to forgive you for not putting your complete trust and hope in Him.

My prayer for you is that you will rise up when you feel like falling.

> Forgive when you give in.
>
> Release when you want to hold on to negativity.
>
> As you clean up your spirit, you heal up your emotional wounds.
>
> As you process your pain in the light of understanding, what was sent to destroy you cannot harm you – if you release it completely to God.
>
> As you release all the bad, hurtful, destructive words spoken over your life, I pray you begin to feel the heaviness of sin move away from you.
>
> As you repent for your weakness of questioning God's promises for you, I believe blessings will begin to be activated within you.
>
> As you see everyone equally, you will appreciate that everything is also for you.
>
> As you let go of feelings of rejection, you will remember that Christ died just for you. In doing so, He unlocked so many more blessings just for you.
>
> As you recognize that there is no need to feel insignificant, unrepresented, denied, damaged, less than, inferior, or unappreciated, you will see the contrast of how special you really are.

I pray that you will finally let go of all the repressed emotions of unworthiness and of low standards; that the God of all truth will be able to heal what is hurting deep inside of you. We have not because we ask not. We settle and hurt ourselves because we fail to step forward in faith and receive the unconditional love God our Heavenly Father has for us. Sometimes we forget that as we reject God's love, we are also rejecting Christ's death on the cross in which He so willingly died without question, and without sin. He knew us who are full of so much sin, yet He gave His life up just for our redemption, salvation, healing, restoration, and victory over so many things we actually struggle with on a daily basis. Abundant living is one of the most common ones; many church folks fail to walk in daily. Please stop this madness of what the Israelites did for forty years, yet in their lesson, they still did not see how God loved them so much. Their shoes never wore out, they never hungered or cried out for thirst. God showed us through their lives how much He loves his children. This is endless, unconditional love…who are we to deny the blessings. God's words say:

> *"Ask, and it shall be given you; seek, and ye shall find; knock, and it shall be opened unto you. For everyone that asketh receiveth; and he that seeketh findeth, and to him that knocketh it shall be opened."* Matthew 7:7-8 (KJV)

This, my Sisters, is your answer to having an Abundant Mindset in Christ.

Anita Sechesky

**Excerpted from *Soul Sister Letters – Let's Talk About Love, Faith, Abundance & Divine Purpose*

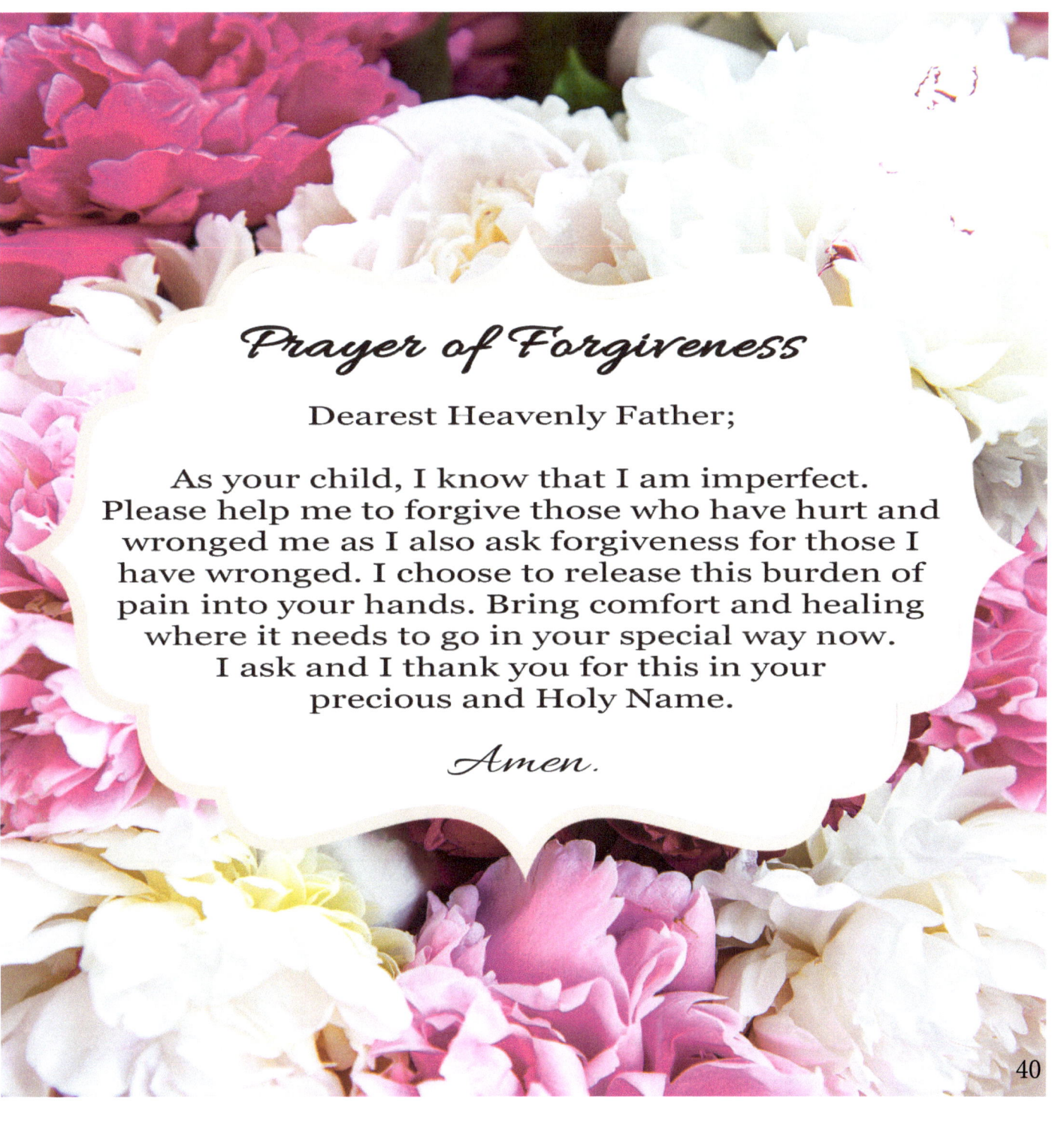

Prayer of Forgiveness

Dearest Heavenly Father;

As your child, I know that I am imperfect. Please help me to forgive those who have hurt and wronged me as I also ask forgiveness for those I have wronged. I choose to release this burden of pain into your hands. Bring comfort and healing where it needs to go in your special way now. I ask and I thank you for this in your precious and Holy Name.

Amen.

Abundance is my birthright as a child of God. I accept every blessing that has my name on it.

—Anita Sechesky

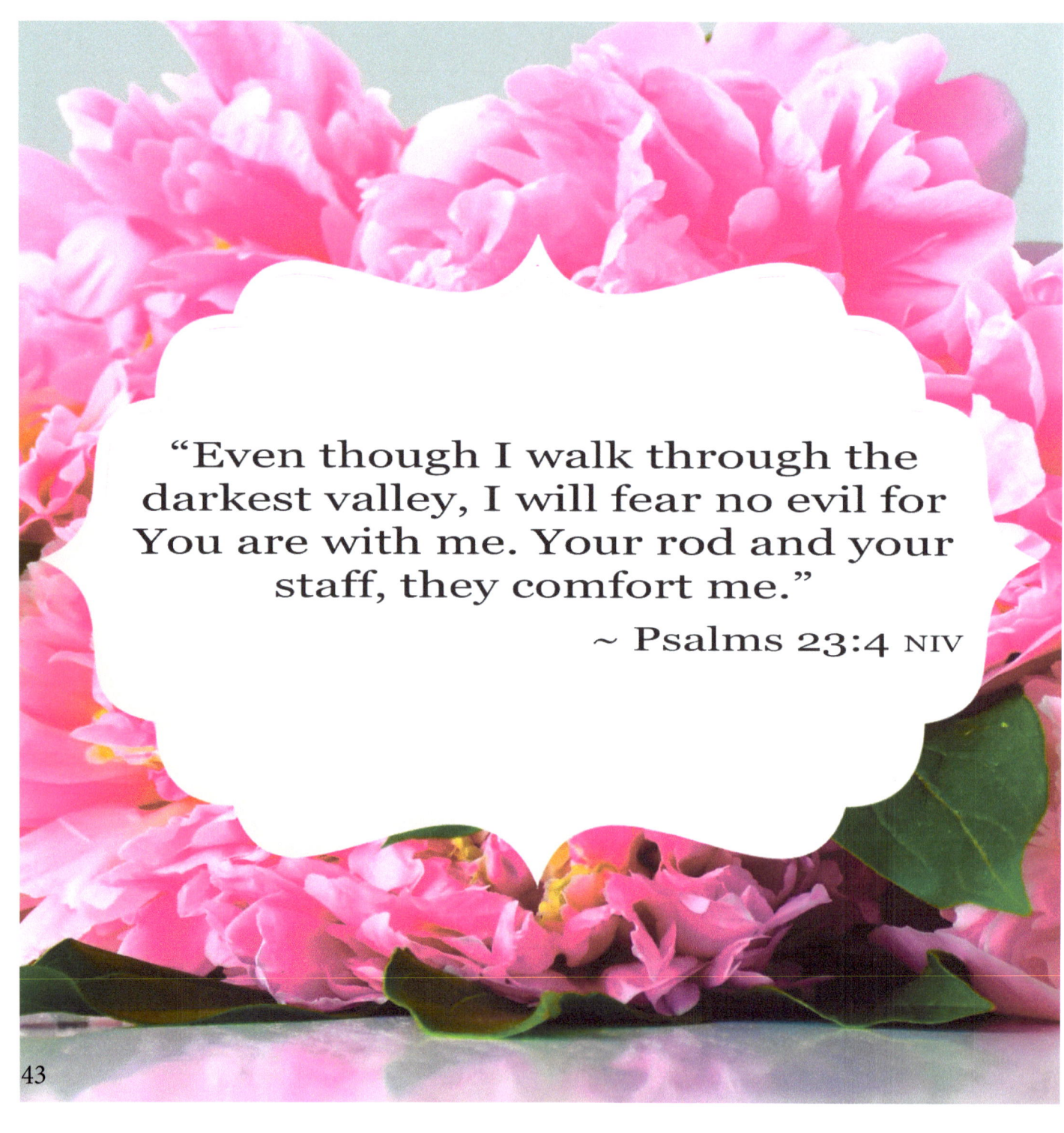

"Even though I walk through the darkest valley, I will fear no evil for You are with me. Your rod and your staff, they comfort me."

~ Psalms 23:4 NIV

Divine Purpose

by Anita Sechesky

Dear Sis; Have you stepped into your divine purpose as yet? You know that feeling that keeps you awake at night. How about those thoughts that you are called for a higher purpose in life? Do you have a special gift and it brings so much joy, healing, or hope to others? Your divine purpose is your ordained God calling. It's all about your expertise and God wants you to use that testimony and make a blessing out of it. Help others; share your story. Maybe you have a gift of baking; then you need to do that thing you want to do. Test it out, take it for a spin by volunteering at the homeless shelter or your church community. You never know where that may lead you. Maybe one day, you will be running your own business and blessing that shelter and all the churches in your area. You get the idea, don't sit on it waiting for something good to show up when it's been inside of you all along. Give yourself the chance to become better. You can do it. You have a gift, and that gift was given to you to use wisely. Do it with intention. Make plans, bring them before the Lord, ask God to bless your plans and to guide you every step of the way. Never do anything without God's blessings; if things go south you decide to blame Him when you never invite your Heavenly Father to oversee anything, to begin with.

Remember, if you are still discovering your divine purpose, you will also know that those same desires were planted in your spirit because God equipped you with those gifts. Although His ways are not our own, God always wants what's best for his children. Stay close to God and many good things will follow you. Although life will not always be easy, you will get through it a lot better than those who don't have our big loving God on their side. Did you know that your life is an example to others? I encourage you, Sis, to continue walking in the anointing of God's covering. His blessings will overtake you and even blow you away. This is the favor of God.

I can't tell you enough how many times I felt so helpless about things in my life, and then God showed up with a solution that shifted my mindset into seeing the bigger picture. I am well aware that God has played a huge role in everything I do. I've learned that despite what others think of me, God still wants to use me for His will to be a blessing to others. It can be in my role as a Registered Nurse, as a Certified Professional Coach and Publisher when I work with my author clients, or just as a regular person. Because God's hands are over my life, I can rest assured that everything I take to Him in prayer, He has already addressed, regardless of what it might be.

Maybe you are still figuring out what your divine purpose is and you haven't had much guidance. I encourage you to find a Bible-believing church that recognizes the gifts of the spirit and the seven-fold ministry. This is where you will be spiritually fed and grow into who you are meant to be.

As for those of you who have carried a vision within your heart for so long, I encourage you to protect that vision by giving it over to God. Ask Him if it is His will for you. Ask him to bless it and wait for the answers because they will come. Ask God to bring in the right people to support and build you up. Be mindful because you will attract snakes who look for what they can get from you. Be careful because you will also meet up with wolves who may try to discourage or scare you. This is when you have something of value. If your enemies are not trying to make things difficult for you, then they see you as one of their own, but if they are troubling you, it's because of what's inside of you and all the plans and purposes that God has declared over your life...the enemy of your soul wants to destroy them.

Your divine purpose is priceless and precious. Remember, if God called you into something, He will give you a unique fingerprint so that you are not like everyone else. You will stand out in the marketplace. You are blessed and highly favored by God. This is the anointing on your life. Embrace it, Sister. There is only one of you and God knows what He was doing and you were created for such a time as this. Walk boldly in faith and let God fight your battles. You will remain blessed and as you take it all to the foot of the cross, allow the blood of Jesus to wash you clean over and over on a daily basis because we must remember that none of us are without sin and to receive the blessings of God, we must remain clean in our spirits. Be filled with Joy as you walk out your divine purpose. This is your God-given destiny. So many Christians sadly miss out on living their divine purpose because they don't have the faith to walk it through. They have allowed the people in their lives to discourage them or they have forgotten that the special gift they have is something that is meant for the greater good. It's not always about your friends and family. Have you thought about that lately? When was the last time you went somewhere and even though you were not meant to be there, you ended up being blessed because of the kindness and generosity of strangers who opened their hearts, homes, and even pocketbooks to bless you unexpectantly? This is what a Divine purpose calling does in someone's life. You become a conduit of abundance. Maybe your services as a business are very focused on customer appreciation so you go out of your way to serve your clients. It doesn't mean that you charge less than what the market value is, nor should you allow others to comprise your value. It means you are an integrity-based business and not like the other service providers across the city who offer similar services but operate in an unethical manner. I've learned as a Christian entrepreneur, that initially I tried to please my customers/clients so much that I literally was giving my publishing services away for free. It was not the wisest thing to do but it was my lack of experience and willingness to please everyone. As time went by, I realized that many other boutique publishers were offering similar services, but charging double, even up to 3x the amount I was charging to unhappy clients. My lesson was to stay true to myself because experience is where real value is placed. I learned the hard way that it's not always easy to please miserable people and that my business is part of my bigger divine purpose which attracts the right people that God brings my way. I will never compromise my gifts anymore. Life lessons will always show what to do and how to correct yourself to protect yourself. Trust the process and allow the Holy Spirit to guide you in all your ways.

I truly believe that we each have a divine purpose and if we feel we don't, then we need to seek God more to hear His voice. What is He saying? What are you called to do? What kind of blessing can you begin to be to those around you? Remember, everyone has a purpose. Everyone has experience. Out of those life lessons, you can see how things unfold for you. Bring everything to the Lord in prayer and don't be discouraged by small beginnings. Every magnificent oak tree was once a small insignificant acorn. Let yourself grow roots in God's word.

My prayer for you is that you'll discover God's will for your life. May you learn how special you really are. May you be healed of past emotions blocking your progress. May your blessings find you and those who are called to walk alongside you show up! Amen!

Anita Sechesky

**Excerpted from *Soul Sister Letters – Let's Talk About Love, Faith, Abundance & Divine Purpose*

Prayer for Peace

Dearest Heavenly Father;

As your child, I come to you because you are a very present help in trouble. Please give me the peace that passeth all understanding and grace to overcome all anxieties and challenges I am going through right now. I ask and I thank you for this in your precious and Holy Name.

Amen.

*You are
creating
the world
around you
by the beauty
in your words.*

-Anita Sechesky

Inspired Living Tip

Looking beyond yourself requires the grace to envision the happiness of others.

~Anita Sechesky

Self-Love & Development

by Anita Sechesky

Dear Sis; How's life treating you lately? I would love to talk to you about Self-Love and Development. I really think it's something we as believers never talk about enough. In fact, I believe that because of the secular world talking about self-love so often and encouraging others to see themselves as God in every sense, Christians tend to shy away from addressing this topic more often than not, contrary to the very fact that we serve a loving God. Our Heavenly Father is a God of love and it's because of his great love for us that some of us are lucky to even be alive. So, tell me what's not to love about a life we have been blessed with regardless of how undeserving we really are? That's how much we are loved. I have come into the understanding that yes, it can be a very fine line as a Christian. Lest we sin and push God out of the picture. But I boldly claim that I am nothing without Christ, and greater is He that's within me than He that's within the world. Again… why would I not love myself if I am created in God's image and God is living inside of me? As we let go of all the things we see as undesirable about ourselves, we are releasing ourselves from the bondage of judgment of others. As we accept every single thing about ourselves, we automatically start accepting everything about every person we meet in life. Self- love is a reflection of what we are, what's inside of us, and it attracts so much more love into our lives endlessly.

Therefore, I encourage you to join me in these positive affirmations:

> YES! I do love myself!
>
> YES! I do love myself!
>
> YES! I do love myself!
>
> YES! I do love and forgive myself!
>
> YES! I do love and forgive myself!
>
> YES! I do love and forgive myself!
>
> YES! I do love and forgive myself so I can create a clean heart and a renewed spirit.
>
> YES! I do love and forgive myself so I can create a clean heart and a renewed spirit.
>
> YES! I do love and forgive myself so I can create a clean heart and a renewed spirit.
>
> YES! I do love and forgive others so I can create a clean heart to encourage myself.
>
> YES! I do love and forgive others so I can create a clean heart to encourage myself.
>
> YES! I do love and forgive others so I can create a clean heart to encourage myself.
>
> YES! I do love, forgive, and encourage myself by the word of God!
>
> YES! I do love, forgive, and encourage myself by the word of God!
>
> YES! I do love, forgive, and encourage myself by the word of God!
>
> YES! I do love and forgive and so I can create a clean heart to encourage myself. YES! I do love, forgive, and encourage myself by God's words to believe that I am a confident, strong, visionary, leader, healer, prayer warrior, and successful woman. I do believe that with God all things are possible for me!

And yes, I often struggle with accepting myself just the way I am. Then I remember what

Jesus did for me. I remember that I can do all things and I know that I have a promise that God will never forsake or abandon me. He is as close as the whisper of His name. I love myself because God loves me; God sent his only son to die for me!!! I love myself because I am far from perfect, but God sees me as precious in his eyes. I love myself because I am forgiven of my sins and without God's forgiveness, I could not bear to deal with that emotional garbage being in my daily presence.

I love myself because I know that I can be used by God to bring glory to His name in the way that I treat others with the loving kindness that God has so freely shown me through His son Jesus and other believers. I am free to forgive myself for thinking I wasn't deserving of God's love because the enemy of my soul wants me to believe that I'm not good enough for God's blessings in my life. So, therefore, that enemy wants me to remain stagnant in my personal development and emotional healing which was a result of sinful living or certain things I attracted into my life because of the wrong choices I have made in the past.

As a result, I have now decided to pursue excellence in all my ways. This means that I hold myself accountable for not living up to the excellence that resides within me. I know that I have already experienced the contrast in non-believers, therefore I am understanding that their negative behaviors toward me were a result of their living in their sinful nature. But as a believer, I have the Holy Spirit present within me at all times, so I am consciously aware of my own shortcomings and strive for excellence in the way that I show up in the world. Choosing to love myself is my first step in recognizing my status as a child of God. I have been adopted into a royal priesthood, so there is no going back to my old ways of living. Why would I throw away the keys to the Kingdom of Heaven? I am blessed because of my association and because of that, my integrity has to be kicked up a notch in the ways that I even view the people around me. I appreciate that it's not my place to judge and with that burden of sin removed from my conduct, I can truly love everyone as they are. I see how our choices can affect the results of our lives, so I am mindful of the things I choose to speak; how I do everything changes because things are just not the same anymore. This is what happens when royalty comes to town. We must present ourselves in our Sunday best. We must believe we are worthy to be present. We must understand that there are conditions to be met to be in the presence of royalty. Therefore, we clean ourselves up to be acceptable in our presentation and conduct. We are so blessed.

What a wonderful life we have, as children of God, to be blessed with His unconditional love. We see through all the clouds and know without a shadow of a doubt our God lives, not just yesterday but today and tomorrow ever after. And because He lives triumphantly, we can face anything that life brings our way. This is how our self-development shifts from being totally independent to being fully dependent on God. It might seem backward to some, but in the believer's perspective, we are even more powerful. We are even more successful. We are even more loved and accepted, and we are blessed and highly favored. I am so grateful to God for the freedom we have in Christ to be just what He has called me to be. The world needs healing and as His hands, we can provide that unconditional healing love. We can become examples to one another. We can become the feet that carry the gospel to the nations. We can walk in faith and know that Love covers a multitude of sins and with that knowledge, there is hope for all.

> *"Love is patient, love is kind. It does not envy, it does not boast, it is not proud. It is not rude, it is not self-seeking, it is not easily angered, it keeps no record of wrongs. Love does not delight in evil but rejoices with the truth."* 1 Corinthians 1:13 (NIV)

Anita Sechesky

**Excerpted from *Soul Sister Letters – Let's Talk About Love, Faith, Abundance & Divine Purpose*

Prayer for Marriage

Dearest Heavenly Father;

I come before you today lifting up my marriage. I ask that you will bless our relationship to be healthy, peaceful and strong. Protect us from falling apart by giving us a unity and bond so that we can overcome temptation, neglect and attacks from the enemy. Guard our hearts to remember why we came together. Please remove anyone from our lives who mean us harm. I release and forgive. I ask and I thank you for this in your precious and Holy Name.

Amen.

My heart beats with Hope and it creates new opportunities for me to prosper and praise my Creator.

-Anita Sechesky

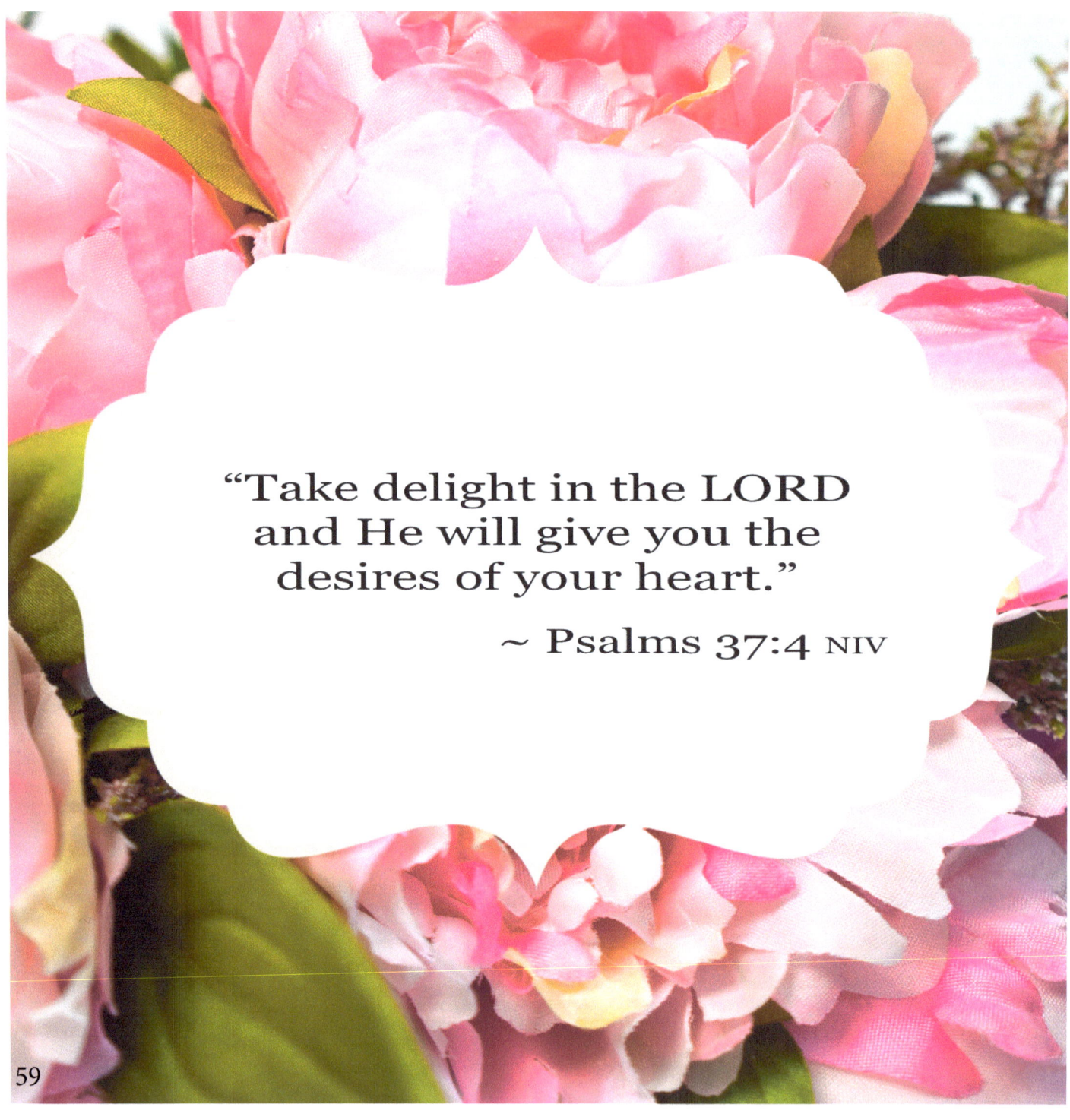

"Take delight in the LORD and He will give you the desires of your heart."

~ Psalms 37:4 NIV

Faith Walk

by Anita Sechesky

Dear Sis; Let's talk about our Faith Walk. If you're like me, you will admit that it's not been an easy journey. This road that we tarry is filled with so many things that test our faith. Then we ask ourselves how we got into situations that we never signed up for! Let me tell you, as a child of God it is not easy. You will grow through your vulnerabilities. You will learn who is real and who is fool's gold. You will shift the way you pray and stand on God's word and promises. Your prayer will become powerful and you will see answers come flooding through. You will experience breakthrough after breakthrough. But it will come with a cost to your comfort zone. You will have to give up that cushy way of handling things and recognize that as a Queen-child of God, the creator of all the heavens and the earth, there is no more room for tolerance. The debt has been paid in full and Jesus' blood has washed your sins away. You are redeemed and You are a free agent to walk in the abundant blessing that your Heavenly Father has said is yours! End of discussion!

We as believers want everything to be just perfect and it can be, but first, we must endure the persecution; we must push past the liars, haters, and mockers who willfully deceive us to our faces. We must cast down vain imaginations that try to set themselves upon us and know that the Victory has been won and the devil is a sore loser. Until that day of redemption, we must proceed with the boldness of being created in the image of Christ our redeemer. We must take up our cross and bear it as we count it all joy because healing is the children's bread. This we can depend on.

We must continue our Faith Walk despite those who fall away. We must encourage others to practice the mindfulness that acknowledges that none of us are perfect but with the daily application of Jesus' precious blood we can confidently wash our sins away. It will bring us closer and closer to that victory of whatever we are facing. It will protect us when we enter into rooms where they may have once spoken badly about us. We must tolerate the ignorance, jealous, and spiteful ways of others without lashing back. We must allow those who sin against us to be placed into God's hands and let Him be our vindicator. We stand on God's word and continually recognize we are so much more than a name, title, and status. We are a blessed child of the highest and living God of Abraham, Isaac, and Jacob. Everything we touch will be blessed to prosper as we walk our faith and talk our faith. We will begin to speak things into existence and yes, we will be able to decree a thing and see it come to pass. Our Faith Walk is powerful once we tap into our source. God is no respecter of persons and what He has done for one He will do for all. So, what's on your heart? Bring it to the foot of the cross. What's troubling you today? Take comfort in knowing that God is already there. Take heart in knowing what troubles you, troubles God and like any parent, God will not tolerate anyone messing with his most precious child. Cry out to God and tell him your woes. Give him the chance to set the record straight. Wait faithfully. Pray without ceasing and don't allow yourself to sin any longer. Set your standards high so you have to leap to appreciate what's waiting for you up there. Keep your heart pure and holy. Walk it out in faith.

Remember, no one said it would be easy, but they did say it will be worth it. Faith without works is dead, meaning you can have all the faith you want but if you speak against your blessings, your prayers will struggle to manifest with the blessings you're expecting. God needs us to be focused on Him as we give Him our worries. Trust Him and watch miracles begin to happen in your life. Pray more for yourself. Pray more for the people in your life, your family, friends, and colleagues. Take the focus off your own situation and lift others up more often. This will create a tidal wave of blessings. As we see what others are facing and selflessly lift them up or come into agreement with them, we are putting tens of thousands of strongholds and wicked thoughts into captivity. We can stand on Psalm 91 and memorize it to become a part of our daily life as we declare God's blessing and protection over ourselves and those we care about. This powerful Psalm, written by King David, covers so many things we still face in this decade. A well-known scripture reads, *"The prayer of a righteous man availeth much."* Well, that's a promise we can stand on to know that we are not wasting our time in prayers. Therefore, we should never cease, until God says so.

I've witnessed so many believers struggle with their identity in Christ because it takes time to build a solid relationship. They go with the premise that God owes them something. They let go of the fact that any relationship worth having must have a commitment from each other. In God's word, He already states his intention towards us many times over. God wants to bless us. God wants to heal us. God wants to prosper us. God wants to restore us and replace what the enemy has stolen from us. And in return, all He asks is for us to love and believe in his one and only son, Jesus, who died for us pitiful, lowly sinners. Yet Jesus was the Prince of Peace. When last have you heard of this ever happening?

I'm not sure if you're facing something that feels uncontrollable and you're feeling like you're backed up against a wall with no way out. Or you may be feeling out of place in a world full of sinners who speak hell and hopelessness into one another's lives. If you're that person, ask yourself WHY?

Faith is a test of our spiritual strength. It causes our weak muscles to be tested and put through things that actually propel us to grow spiritually. Not everyone is trustworthy but eager to get into our business. Pray for discernment so that you can smell the enemy before he dares enter into your presence. This is only a snip of what it means to be a child of God. People will try to break your faith, but it's only you that needs to appreciate the significance of what it all means to be a child of the Most High and loving God.

Why would you choose to step away from being in the center of God's will and attention?

Why aren't you ready to release the conceitedness that's been etched on your soul? Understand this, Sister, it appears that there is some deep emotional healing that must be addressed because it's tainting our spirits. It is influencing how others perceive us. It will cause us to feel shame, guilt, anger, and even hate towards those who care more about us. There's nothing wrong with acknowledging your parents to the ends of the earth – how do we acknowledge God our heavenly Father, if we ignore and hold offenses against our earthly father? Forgive, forgive, and forgive once again. Don't ever be shy about choosing the act of forgiveness. As we walk in this direction and standard, we are releasing and setting free the locked-up blessings over our lives. This is a test of faith because if there was no solid or healthy relationship, much less friendship amongst one another, it would still be hard to forgive.

Regardless of your relationship issues, job situations, health status, or financial security, I implore you to walk it out without hesitation. You will get your answers. God will never leave you nor will He forsake you. This powerful journey will make you stronger than you have ever been, as long as you never compromise your position in Christ. Faith is something we must carry within us so that what we believe is manifested quickly and with ease into our lives. Faith holds no records of our wrongs; it is an action word that requires us to act in accordance with confident expectations. It doesn't say to focus on the delay but instead, it is empowered even more by the usage of power phrases such as "without delay" or "immediately." I encourage us all to never forget the power of Faith and how our prayers were answered in the past. It should be enough to make believers out of us all over again.

Anita Sechesky

**Excerpted from *Soul Sister Letters – Let's Talk About Love, Faith, Abundance & Divine Purpose*

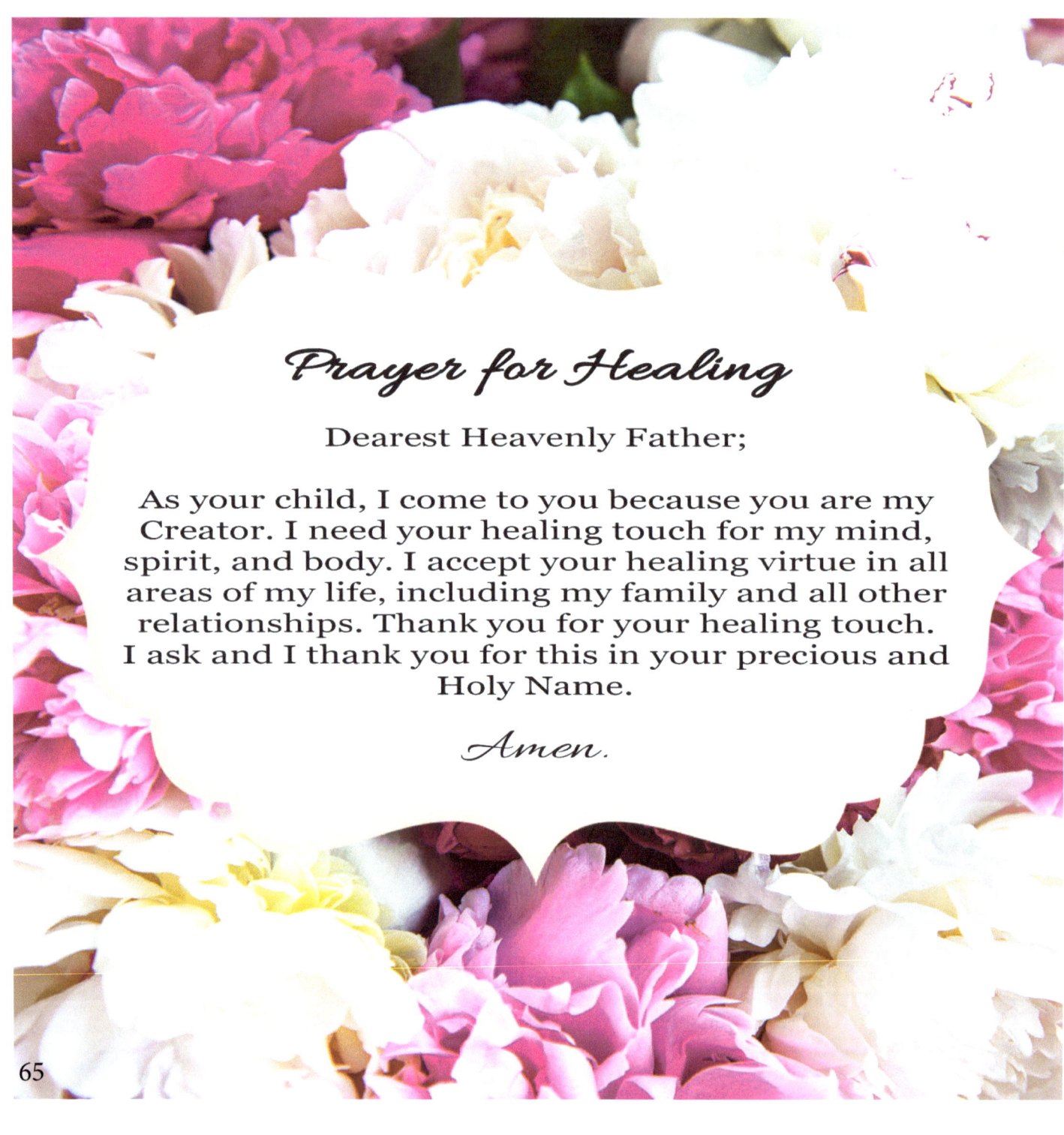

Prayer for Healing

Dearest Heavenly Father;

As your child, I come to you because you are my Creator. I need your healing touch for my mind, spirit, and body. I accept your healing virtue in all areas of my life, including my family and all other relationships. Thank you for your healing touch. I ask and I thank you for this in your precious and Holy Name.

Amen.

You can turn your mistakes into opportunities to shift your perception and determine new approaches in life.
~Anita Sechesky

No Greater Love

by Anita Sechesky

Everyone wants to believe that there is hope in this life despite the circumstances they may be facing. We all want to know that there are answers to the questions that seem impossible and hard to comprehend. Life is not always easy and oftentimes the challenges we walk through can leave a person feeling disempowered and discouraged. The thought of there being some sort of spiritual intervention bringing hope, healing, and a little faith to even believe that things will become better if we only believe and walk in an attitude of gratitude and appreciation is more than many could even imagine; some might even say fictional and far-fetched. There are still those who choose to remain "in the dark" when it comes to stories of God's Heavenly Angels being a part of our everyday lives. We even forget how there have been biblical stories of Angels appearing to mankind long ago to bring warnings, encouragement, and even protection around those they revealed themselves to.

As an individual who has worked in health care for over twenty-five years, I have heard many stories from colleagues and patients about Angels that have been known to bring comfort and inspiration to those who believe. I feel I was very blessed to have my own Angel experience after the loss of my first child. My daughter Jasmine Rose was full-term and born sleeping. It was a difficult time for me, and I had gone through a period where it was next to impossible to even talk about it. I couldn't even pray and asked my husband

and mom to pray on my behalf as my heart was filled with so much grief and anxiety. I had completely lost my self-expression to inconsolable tears and heartache because her death was so unexpected. It all unfolded at the time when she was supposed to be swaddled up to come home and live as a little person with her mommy and daddy. Instead, she was born by induction on a busy maternity floor during the height of the Christmas holidays and just days before my birthday. I don't know which part of that experience was worse than the other. Was it seeing the massive knots in her umbilical cord after her birth, and knowing in my heart that I intuitively knew that weeks before? If only someone would have listened to me that something was wrong, Jasmine would have been in my arms that day looking up into my eyes. Or was it the moment when the nurses told me to go for a walk and stretch my legs? And as I walked down that long hallway, it felt as if everyone was reading a sign over my head that I was a childless mommy. They were taking their babies home while I had to go bury mine.

As the weeks went by, the crying changed to fear and then to nightmares. In hindsight, I realize that I entered into a season of Post-Traumatic Stress Disorder. I had no professional support, as my small hometown community did not have a support group in place, although my Physician encouraged me to start a special group for other grieving parents. My hometown had a number of families who had also suffered a similar tragedy. Obviously, I was not ready at that time of my life to take on such a responsibility – I was also walking through that horrific ordeal. My husband dealt with his grief quietly, although he was very supportive of me.

Sometime after our daughter's burial, I started having very disturbing evil dreams that left me terrified and feeling even more helpless and isolated. One particular night I was sitting up in bed reading, and out of the "corner of my eye," I got a glimpse of something that completely changed the way I perceived life and that we are living in a world that is multi-dimensional where there are supernatural beings around us, even though we may not see them with our natural eyes. At that moment I witnessed the most astounding sight – right in front of me in full view for that brief second. Although it was not my first supernatural experience, this time it was the opposite that brought comfort and peace around me. I saw the biggest, most beautiful and plushest wings that were swooping down across the bedroom floor, the feathers were of the lushest plumes I have ever seen. I saw arms, the biggest arms with muscles that were formed, flexed, folded across and very developed, and a strong male chest. I saw a Roman skirt with long leather pleats. I saw the leather sandals that were laced up two very strong legs. I saw the sword that was strapped across the chest and hanging to the left side of his body. The blade on the sword was huge and heavy. And then I saw the face of this Angel man. It was the face of a baby, just like a cherub, gentle and yet stern. The look on the face was peaceful and confident. He was on guard at the end of my bedroom, protecting me. My world instantly shifted to understand that I was not alone. God indeed cared for me and He sent his very best to protect and watch over me, despite how fearful I was feeling. I never did have another bad dream again after that night.

There are many times in my life I wondered if there truly was a God, and did he really care about me? I am so far from perfect. I make mistakes all the time. I don't know why Jesus would die for me. I am a nobody. I wasn't born into a wealthy family and haven't made any life-changing discoveries. I don't have a tribe of people around me. I don't think I'm anything special. As I write this chapter, the Easter season is approaching and many people will be off on holidays, celebrating a long weekend with their loved ones and friends. But I really wonder how many people will stop to think of the gentle man called Jesus who was the peaceful storyteller, peacemaker, friend, brother, son. I wonder if they knew His real story and how His life was sacrificed so that one day all the nobodies, somebodies, and those who even consider themselves higher than that, can actually choose where they will spend all of eternity after their time has expired on this earth. I wonder why people scorned him, yet He was so perfect. He never hurt a single hair on anyone. He never lied. He never stole. He never cheated. He never abused anyone. He never took anyone for granted. He never disrespected anyone. He was not a drunk. He was not a drug addict. He was not a lustful man. He was not a fraud. He was not a wife-beater. He was not a delinquent father. He was not a rapist. He was not a child abuser. He was not scandalous. He was not a gossiper. He was not self-seeking. He was not an opportunist. He was not a gambler. He was not a vandal. He was not a murderer. He was not dirty. He was not wasteful. He was not loud and obnoxious. He was not stingy. He was not vengeful. He was not hot-tempered. He was not full of rage. He was not jealous. He was not controlling. He was not a scammer. He was not a liar. He was not spiteful. He did not hurt His parents. He kept His word. He was a good son. He was a good citizen. He was a good friend. He was a good craftsman. He was caring, kind, empathetic, forgiving, thoughtful, trustworthy, humble and meek. He never forgot the poor, the sick, the young, the old, and the destitute.

YET...they hated Him all of a sudden because of their own pride, ego, hate, jealousy, revenge, and most of all, their fear of the omnipotence that came from the heavenly throne of God and the royalty that surrounded His very presence. Jesus shifted the atmosphere because His vibration of purity, love, and peace was so untouchable, lives were changed in His presence. His integrity could not be shaken, beaten, or destroyed, right up to His last breath when He called out, "It is finished!" Where can you find a person that can love you so much that would give up his life? His good life, up until that moment, had been lived with joy and serving His people. He had loyal followers, a family that loved Him, and a career He enjoyed. Yet when called for service, never did He say, "No. I don't know her. I don't know him. Why should I die for them? Look at all the destructive ways they have lived their lives, while I didn't. Why should I die for them?" Instead, He humbly endured the persecution, humility, shame, pain, disgrace, and abuse that should have been for all the sinners who sinned. He who was free of sin took the sin of the whole world on His back, never looking back. What greater love could there be? When His blood hit the face of this earth, the world as humanity in that day and age changed for all of eternity. His blood was shed for all our sins. We who don't deserve, yet He served His life for our redemption, our healing. Our hope is built on nothing more solid, strong, death-defying, disease-curing, life-changing, purifying blood of Jesus. The blood without impurities. The blood that broke the chains off your life.

So today, I ask you, have you found someone who would do that for you? If not, I would like to introduce you to my best friend, Jesus. Your life will never be the same. No counselor, coach, pastor, preacher, priest, apostle, teacher, or leader could ever measure up and one day, they will all look to Him for their salvation as well. I encourage you to find a Bible-believing church that recognizes the seven-fold ministry: Father, Son, and Holy Spirit. It is well. Amen.

Anita Sechesky

**Excerpted from *Love Your Life – Inspiration to Motivate You for Living a Life Without Limitations*

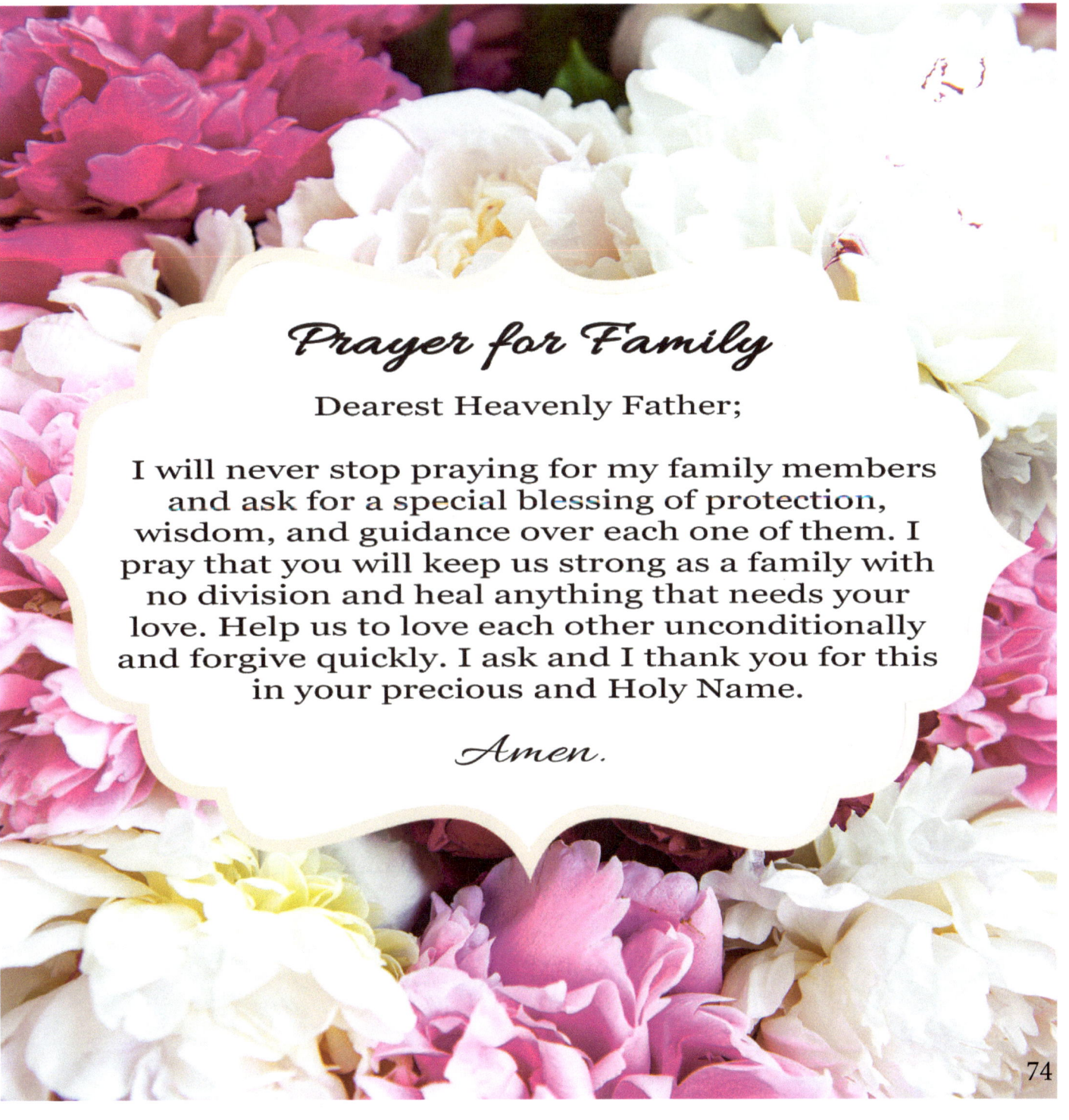

Prayer for Family

Dearest Heavenly Father;

I will never stop praying for my family members and ask for a special blessing of protection, wisdom, and guidance over each one of them. I pray that you will keep us strong as a family with no division and heal anything that needs your love. Help us to love each other unconditionally and forgive quickly. I ask and I thank you for this in your precious and Holy Name.

Amen.

My life is a miracle and I choose to see miracles everywhere around me.

—Anita Sechesky

You are far more precious than jewels

Proverbs 31:10

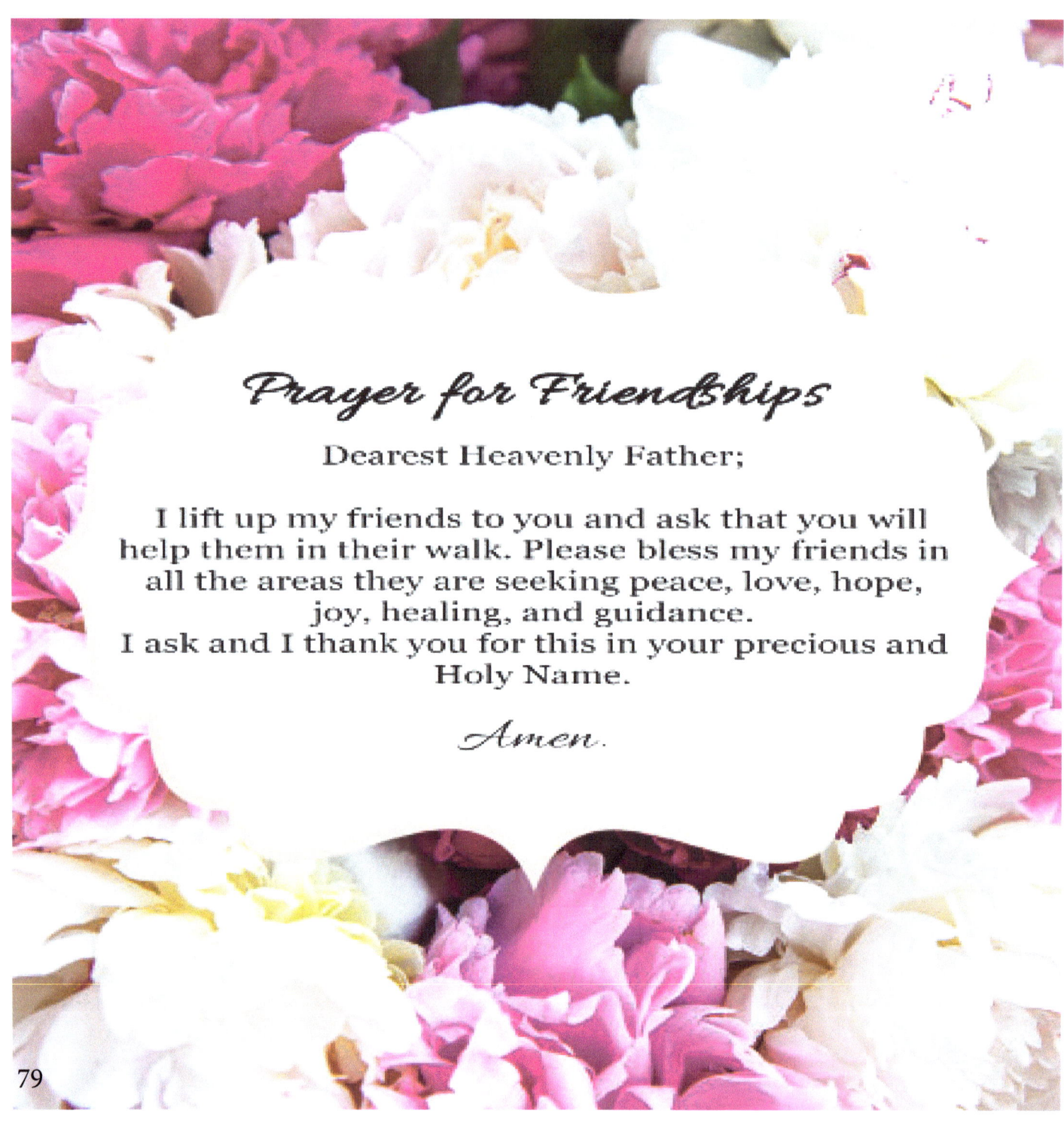

Prayer for Friendships

Dearest Heavenly Father;

I lift up my friends to you and ask that you will help them in their walk. Please bless my friends in all the areas they are seeking peace, love, hope, joy, healing, and guidance.
I ask and I thank you for this in your precious and Holy Name.

Amen.

Success happens when you empower your mind and see the greatness within yourself.

~Anita Sechesky

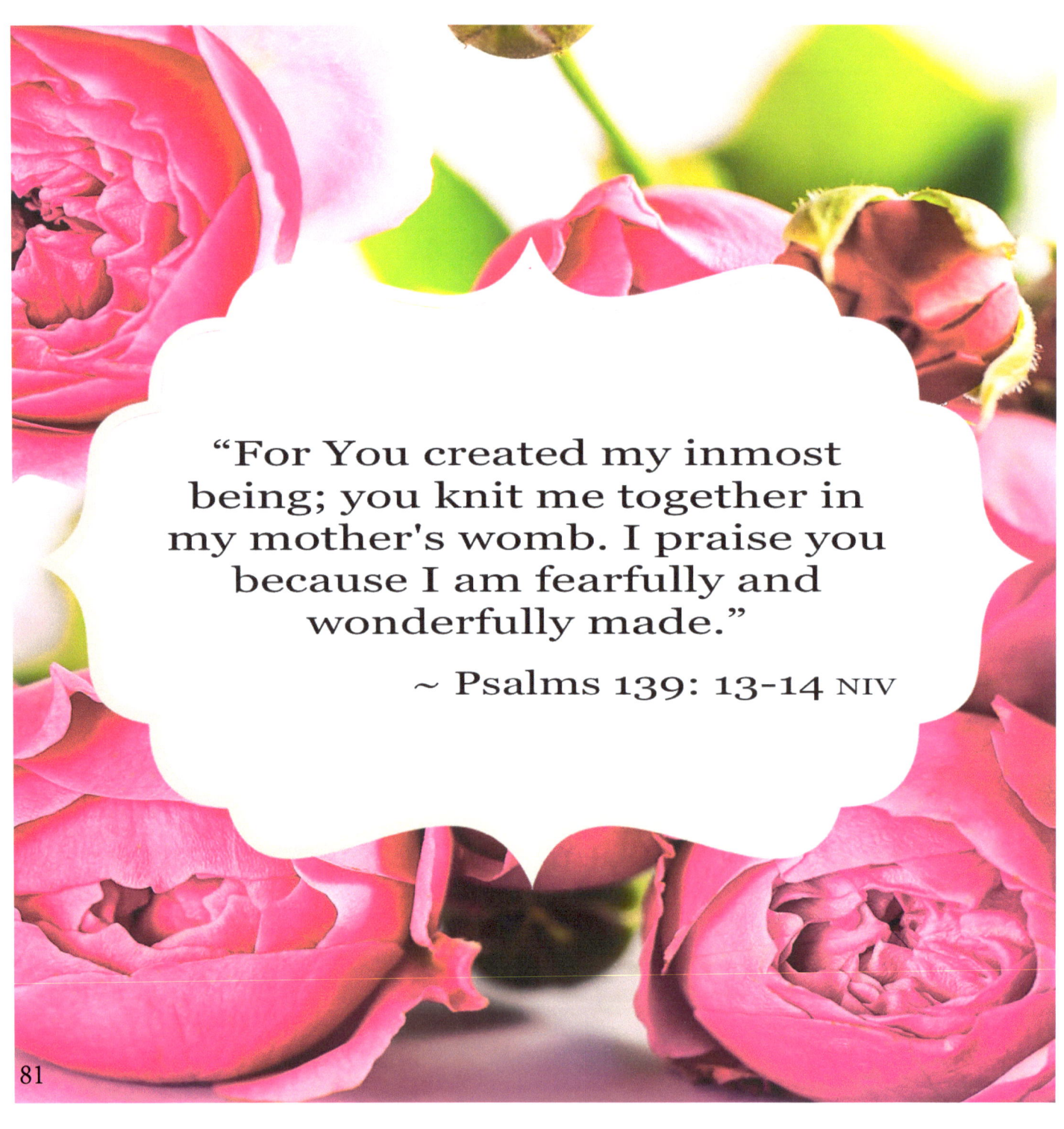

"For You created my inmost being; you knit me together in my mother's womb. I praise you because I am fearfully and wonderfully made."

~ Psalms 139: 13-14 NIV

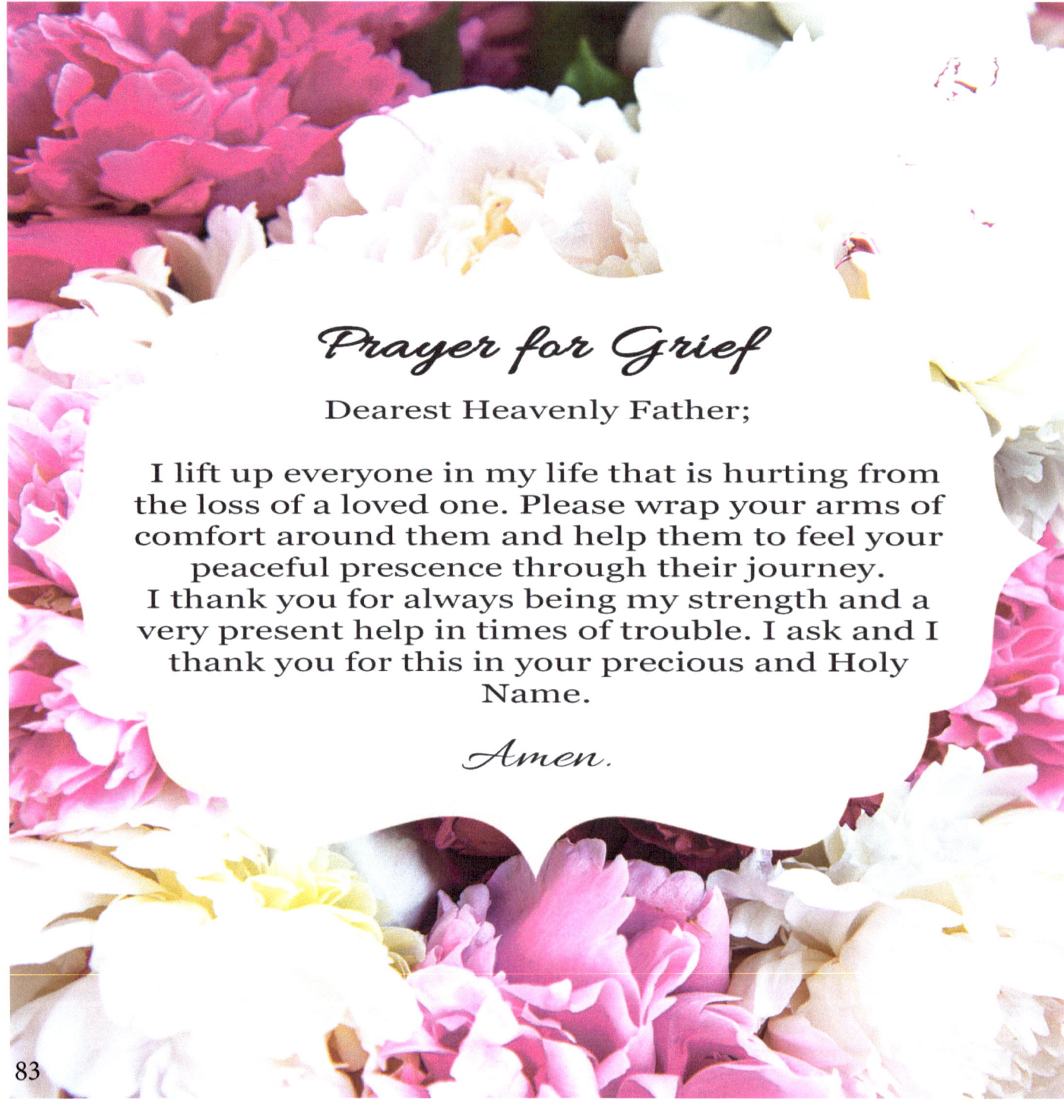

Prayer for Grief

Dearest Heavenly Father;

I lift up everyone in my life that is hurting from the loss of a loved one. Please wrap your arms of comfort around them and help them to feel your peaceful prescence through their journey.
I thank you for always being my strength and a very present help in times of trouble. I ask and I thank you for this in your precious and Holy Name.

Amen.

You are not the limitations that people place on you. You are exactly who you choose to become.

—Anita Sechesky

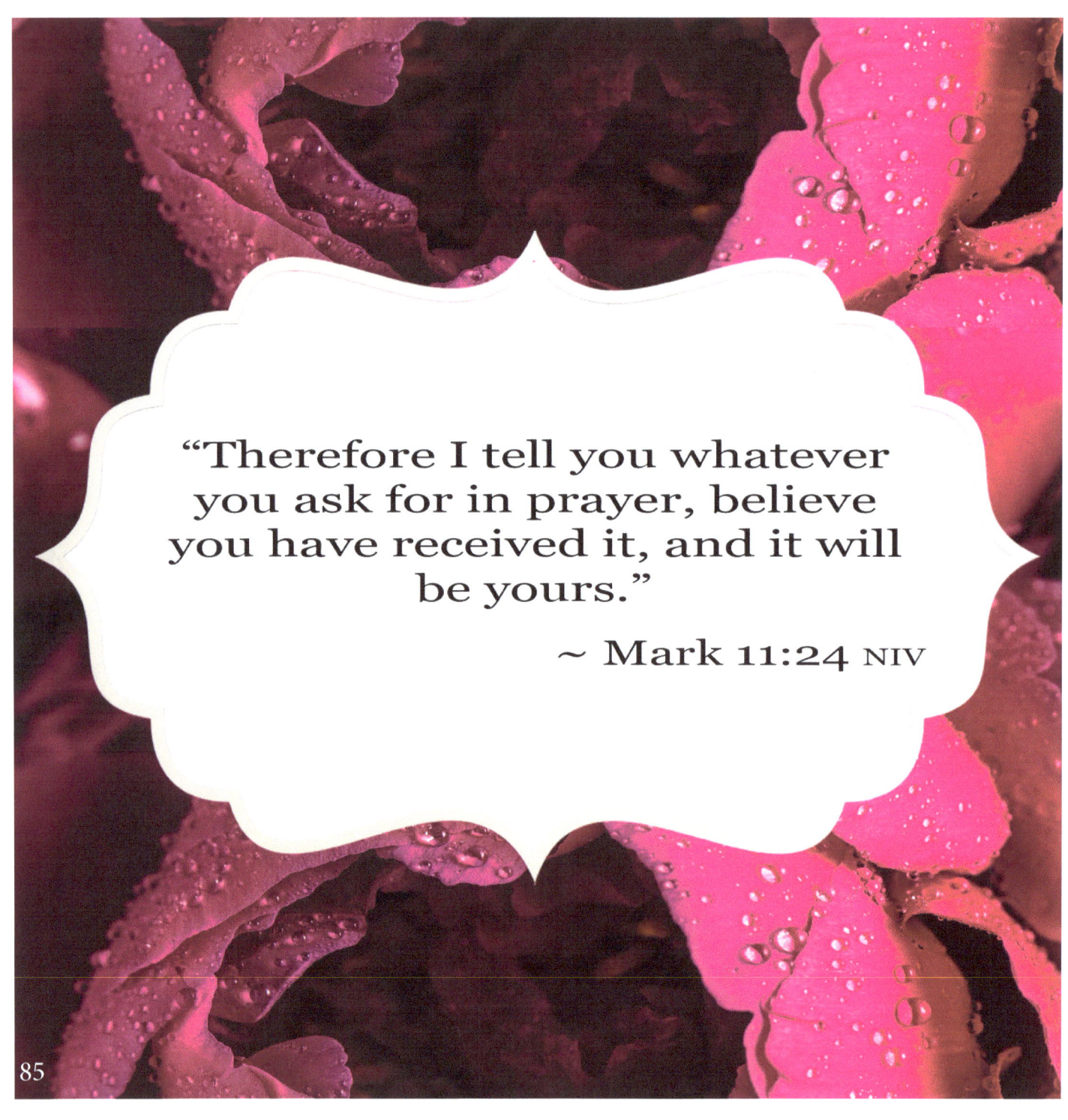

"Therefore I tell you whatever you ask for in prayer, believe you have received it, and it will be yours."

~ Mark 11:24 NIV

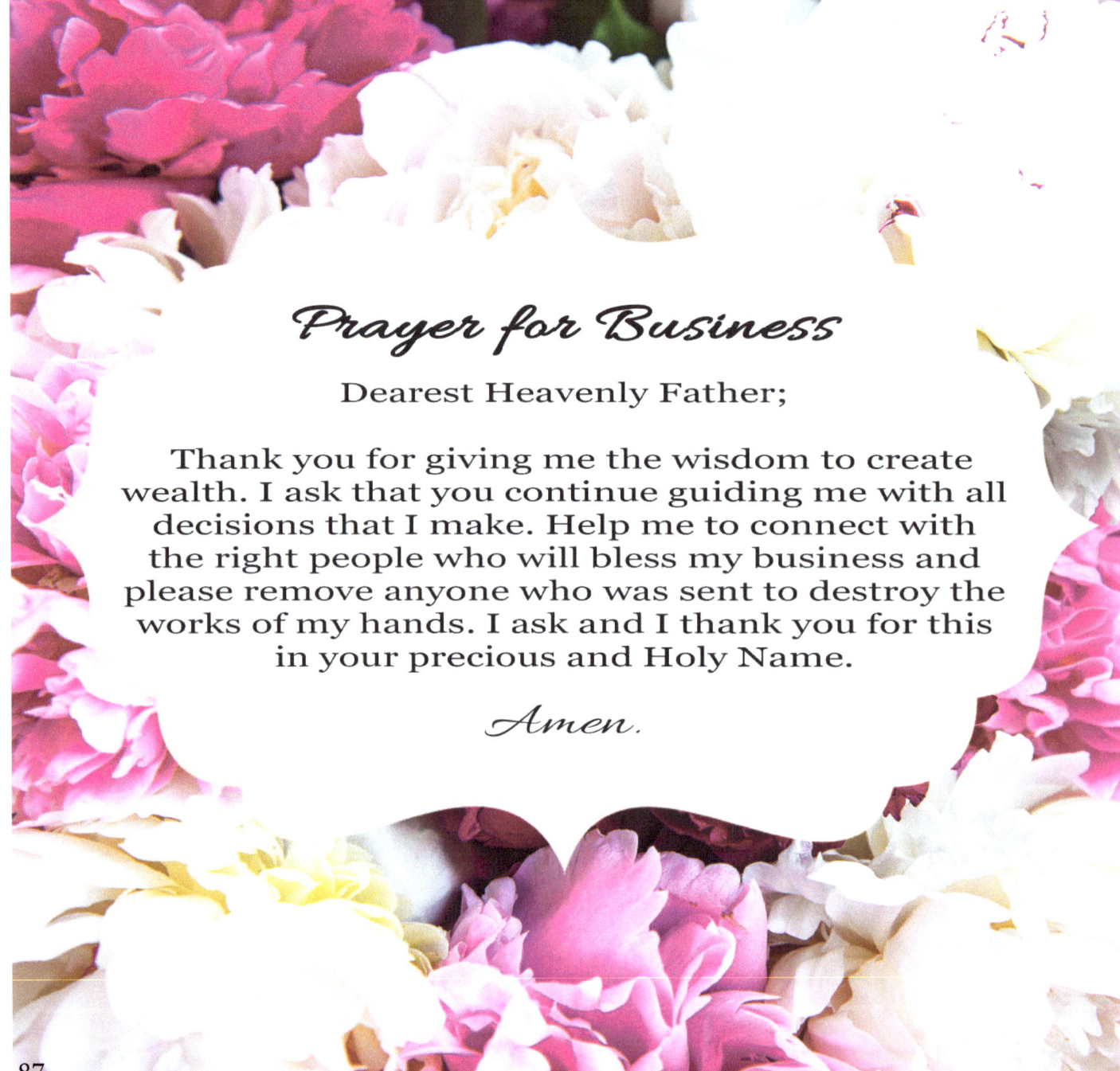

Prayer for Business

Dearest Heavenly Father;

Thank you for giving me the wisdom to create wealth. I ask that you continue guiding me with all decisions that I make. Help me to connect with the right people who will bless my business and please remove anyone who was sent to destroy the works of my hands. I ask and I thank you for this in your precious and Holy Name.

Amen.

Humanity is an extension of who you are. Choose to accept and believe in everyone, not just your own

~Anita Sechesky

About The Author

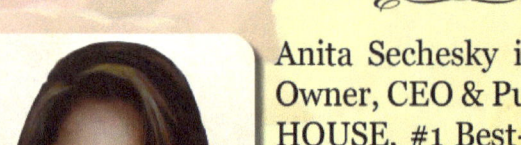

Anita Sechesky is an RN, ICF-CPC, Founder, Owner, CEO & Publisher at LWL PUBLISHING HOUSE, #1 Best-Selling Author, Book Writing Coach, Ghost Writer, Keynote Speaker, Workshop & Conference Host, and the INSPIRED TO WRITE Podcast Host.

Anita is the author of multiple Best-Selling books in the Faith, Inspirational Self-Healing, positive psychology genres, and children's literature as well as a Motivational Keynote Speaker and Mentor. She has successfully published over 580 authors, enjoys hosting INSPIRED TO WRITE workshops, facilitates Masterclasses on Emotional Healing, and speaking at events that focus on living your best life possible. Anita has worked in many Emergency Rooms and health care facilities all over Ontario and has witnessed how one's emotional well-being can impact the human spirit, health and wellness, relationships, and overall potential. It is her greatest desire to promote healing of not only the body, but also the mind and spirit of each man, woman, and child through her vision.

Inspire the World with Us

If you would like to have Anita speak at your event or organization, or if you are interested in writing your own inspired story and would like to work with Anita to help you bring your best efforts forward to publication, please contact her below.

Lastly, if you are interested in joining one of her Masterclasses on Emotional Healing, please visit our website and subscribe to our mailing list to stay updated on future events.

Website: www.lwlpublishinghouse.com
Email: lwlclienthelp@gmail.com

TAKE INSPIRED ACTION IN 2021
Written by: Anita Sechesky

Available in Full Color or B&W on Amazon

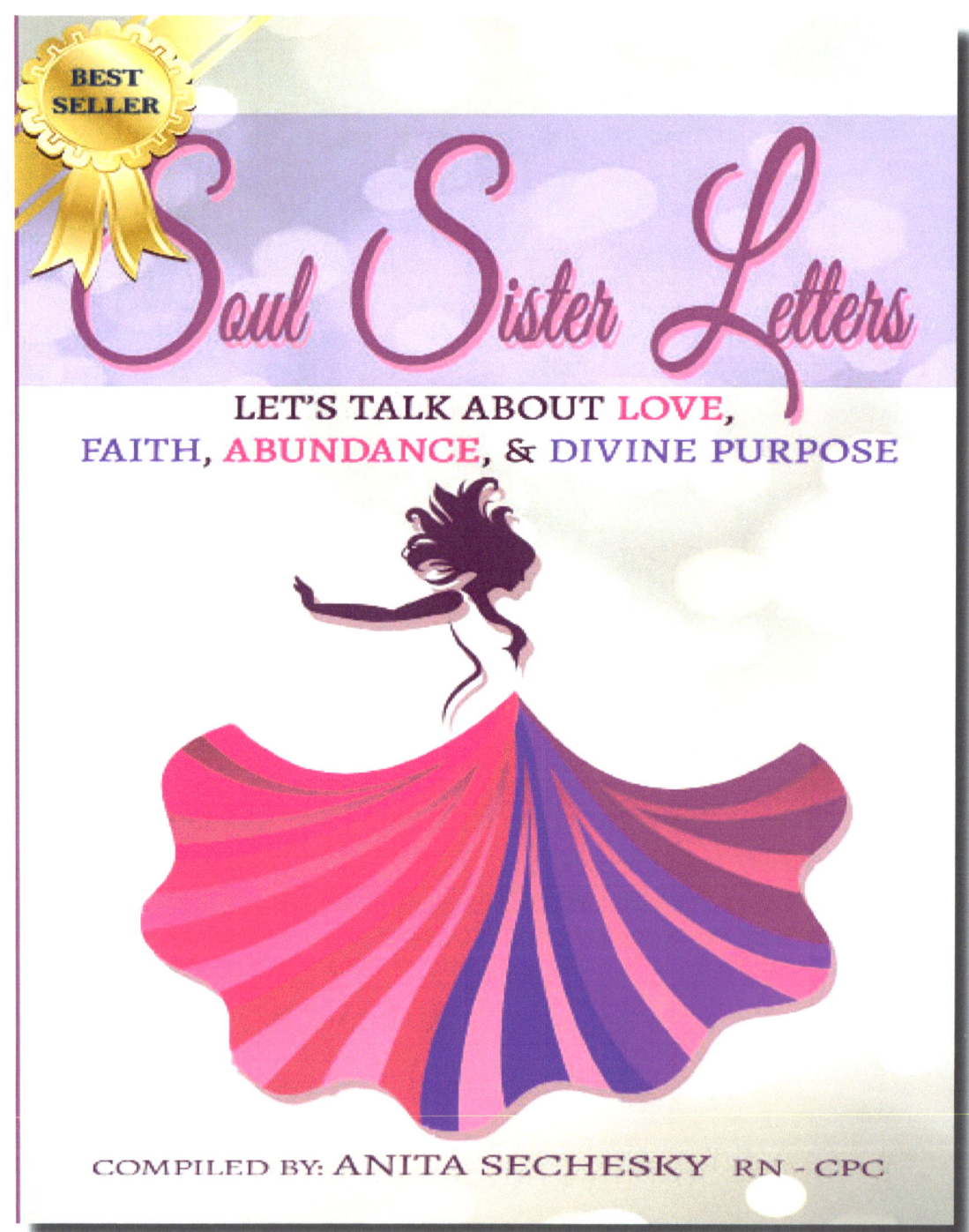

www.ingramcontent.com/pod-product-compliance
Lightning Source LLC
Chambersburg PA
CBHW041452020526
44114CB00054B/69